lonely planet

POCKET
MONTRÉAL &
QUÉBEC CITY

John Garry

Contents

Plan Your Trip 4

The Journey Begins Here 4
Our Picks 6
Perfect Days 16
Get Prepared 20
When To Go 22
Getting There 24
Getting Around 25
 A Few Surprises 28

Top: Gate to Chinatown (p63), Montréal
Bottom: Basilique Notre-Dame (p38), Montréal

POCKET MONTRÉAL & QUÉBEC CITY

Explore Montréal & Québec City — 33

Old Montréal	35
Downtown & Chinatown	55
Quartier Latin, the Village & HoMa	73
Plateau Mont-Royal	87
Mile End, Little Italy & Outremont	101
Lachine Canal & Southwest Montréal	115
Québec City	127
Île d'Orléans	146
Parc de la Chute-Montmorency	148
Wendake	150

Montréal & Québec City Toolkit — 153

Family Travel	154
Accomodations	155
Food, Drink & Nightlife	156
LGBTIQ+ Travelers	158
Health & Safe Travel	159
Responsible Travel	160
Accessible Travel	162
Nuts & Bolts	163
Language	164
Index	166

★ Top Experiences

Basilique Notre-Dame	38
Old Port	39
Parc Jean-Drapeau	50
Musée des beaux-arts de Montréal	58
Parc Olympique & Espace pour la vie	76
Parc du Mont-Royal	90
Cycle to Île de la Visitation	104
Fortifications de Québec	130
Musée de la Civilisation	131

FROM TOP LEFT: SUN_SHINE/SHUTTERSTOCK, GEORGE PACHANTOURIS/GETTY IMAGES

Lonely Planet respectfully acknowledges that Canada is the traditional territory of more than 630 First Nations communities as well as Inuit and Métis communities. We offer gratitude to the Indigenous Peoples for their care for, and teachings about, this land.

The Journey Begins Here

Montréal has a split personality. It's a linguistic mélange of French and English; the sacred 'City of a Hundred Steeples' and sacrilegious 'Sin City' of Prohibition-era revelry. Old Montréal feels like a European village; Downtown's skyscrapers epitomize North American modernity. It's Québécois pride and immigrant ingenuity. It's snow-slammed winters and sweltering summers. With so much variety, choosing sides can be tempting, like pledging loyalty to your favorite MTL bagel bakery. But you don't have to choose. Montréal lets you have it all – and that includes nearby Québec City, a sprinkling of old-world Europe in Canada.

John Garry
@garryjohnfrancis
John is a travel writer, teacher, urban wanderer, foodie and museum devotee, credited in a dozen Lonely Planet guides.

Montréal in autumn
AJANSEN/GETTY IMAGES

THE BEST

Green Space Experiences

With nearly 2000 parks, Montréal and Québec City clearly agree – getting outside is essential. Join locals in their public backyards, each reflecting what the Québécois prize: natural beauty, local terroir and fields fit for a big fête.

Climb to Parc du Mont-Royal's **Belvédère Kondiaronk** (p90; pictured) for a breathtaking panorama of Downtown Montréal's skyscraper forest.

Sail across the St Lawrence to **Parc Jean-Drapeau** (p50) for cityscape views, summer dance parties and Expo 67 relics on a human-made island.

Cycle the **Lachine Canal** (p115) a 19th-century industrial waterway beautified into parks and pretty paths.

Cool off in summer by wading into the gentle waters around **Plage de Verdun** (p122), lapped by the St Lawrence River.

Feel the power of Québec's tallest waterfall while crossing a suspension bridge at **Parc de la Chute-Montmorency** (p148).

Zoom by vineyards, organic farms and flower gardens along **Île d'Orléans** (p146; pictured) with distant views of Québec City.

Right: Chute de Montmorency (p148), Québec City

FROM LEFT: EVA BLUE/COURTESY TOURISME MONTRÉAL/LONELY PLANET, DELPIXEL/SHUTTERSTOCK, JULIE AUDET, SÉPAQ/LONELY PLANET

THE BEST
Winter Experiences

When the weather outside is frosty, the Québécois bundle up to embrace the glittering snowscape. Frozen ponds become ice-skating rinks, public parks turn into snowshoeing courses and festivals in both cities celebrate the snowy season.

Lace up ice skates or don cross-country skis to glide around snow-dusted trails throughout **Parc Jean-Drapeau** (p50).

Grab a toboggan and zoom down Québec City's **Glissade de la Terrasse** (p138), reaching speeds of up to 70km/h.

Soak in saunas, steam rooms and hot tubs aboard Montréal's **Bota Bota** (p46; pictured), a floating spa moored in the icy St Lawrence.

Don a colorful snowsuit to step touch through the night at **Igloofest** (p139; pictured), an outdoor EDM festival in Montréal and Québec City.

Participate in **Carnaval de Québec** (p138) three weeks of ice-tastic festivities in Québec City.

Avoid Montréal's coldest days by exploring the underground tunnels of **Réseau de la Ville Souterraine** (RÉSO; p68).

Right: Snow slides, Parc Jean-Drapeau (p50), Montréal

PLAN YOUR TRIP

THE BEST

Art Experiences

Québec is decorated with more than 3500 public artworks, 200-plus galleries and dozens of museums, its list of artistic superlatives stretching on longer than a Celine Dion power ballad. The arts are embedded in its provincial DNA.

Reserve several hours to explore the trove of classical masterpieces and modern installations inside **Musée des Beaux-Arts de Montréal** (p58; pictured).

Search Plateau Mont-Royal's alleys to find its **remarkable murals** (p92) – or join Spade and Palacio's exceptional street art tour.

Pop into Mile End's **contemporary art galleries** (p109), including a mural-covered stairwell and the city's first Indigenous artist–run showroom.

Get to know some of Québec's best contemporary painters, including Jean-Paul Riopelle, at the **Musée National des beaux-arts du Québec** (p140).

Be inspired by the visionary artists at **PHI** (p46), bringing multisensory magic to Old Montréal with free-to-visit exhibits.

Learn about Québec's Indigenous history at the architecturally stunning **Musée de la Civilisation** (p131; pictured).

Right: Musée National des beaux-arts du Québec (p140), Québec City

PLAN YOUR TRIP

THE BEST
Architecture Experiences

Québec's cityscapes span four centuries of urban evolution. From cobblestone streets lined with Victorian facades to 19th-century industrial landmarks and 20th-century remnants from Expo 67, every block has a story to tell.

Sit back for the psychedelic AURA Experience light show, spotlighting the Gothic Revival interior of Old Montréal's **Basilique Notre-Dame** (p38).

Hop between the 19th-century buildings, such as Hotel Mount Stephen (pictured), that decorate the **Golden Square Mile** (p60), once the stomping ground of Canada's industrial-era ruling class.

Book a tour of architect Moshe Safdie's modular masterpiece **Habitat 67** (p120), his Brutalist design for Expo 67.

Walk the imposing stone **fortification walls** (p130) hugging the city to see Old Québec from a colonial soldier's point of view.

Twirl around **Place Royale** (p134), eyeing centuries-old stone homes with mansard roofs rising from Québec City's cobblestone streets.

Step inside **Château Frontenac** (p135; pictured), Québec City's skyline icon, to appreciate the elegant lobby dripping with old-world grandeur.

THE BEST
Sidewalk Experiences

From the fairy-tale charm of Québec City's oldest roads to the serenity of Montréal's green alleys, joining the pedestrian parade is a fantastic way to uncover both cities' souls.

Experience the multicultural cacophony of **Blvd St-Laurent** (p94), where over a century's worth of immigrants built new lives in Québec.

Head down **Ave Duluth** (p95) in summer, when the street closes to traffic and pedestrians wander from independent shops to restaurant terraces.

Shop along Rue Ste-Catherine's Downtown stretch by day, then bop between **LGBTIQ+ bars** (p85) along its Village strip at night.

Take your pick on **Rue Wellington** (p122), one of the hippest streets in Montréal: perhaps brasseries, comic art, clothes or cafes.

Skip along **Rue du Petit-Champlain** (p134; pictured), the oldest commercial street in Canada, packed with artisan shops and restaurants.

Dine and drink down **Rue St-Jean** (p141), St-Jean-Baptiste's main artery, to experience Québec City's contemporary side.

Petit-Champlain (p134), Québec City

THE BEST

Culinary Experiences

Get to know Québec through its belly. The province blends French finesse and global influences with a budding locavore movement prizing regional farm fare. It's hearty as poutine and sweet as maple syrup – prepare to indulge.

Flit between food stands at Montréal's **Marché Jean-Talon** (p110; pictured) and **Marché Atwater** (p120), where shoppers hunt for farm-grown treats.

Make a reservation at **Vin Mon Lapin** (p111), a French-Italian bistro with a menu featuring seasonal produce and natural wines.

Eat your way through **Mile End** (p108) at tiny shops hocking hand-held snacks – a toothsome representation of the neighborhood's multicultural melting pot.

Choose from over 30 styles of poutine at **La Banquise** (p97), the legendary 24/7 mess-plate palace going strong since 1968.

Taste the difference between bagels at **Fairmount** and **St-Viateur** (p108) so you can argue with Montréalers about who does it better.

Get the full maple-drenched sugar shack experience with traditional Québécois classics at **La Bûche** (p143; pictured) in Québec City.

FROM LEFT: BONDARENCO VLADIMIR/SHUTTERSTOCK, ANDRIY BLOKHIN/ALAMY

Best for Kids

Ride the observation wheel, swing through the pirate-themed park and catch an IMAX science movie around Montréal's **Old Port** (p39).

Dive into history at **Pointe-à-Callière** (p44), where kids can join a simulated archaeological dig above 17th-century foundations.

Waddle with penguins and wave at river otters while wandering through five ecosystems under one roof at the **Biodôme** (p77). Make it a full day by flitting with the **Insectarium**'s (p79) butterflies.

Rent snow tubes to race down the hill above Montréal's **Lac aux Castors** (p90) or don skates to zip around the neighboring ice rink.

Fill up on chocolate truffles – plus ice cream in summer and hot cocoa in winter – at the **Chocolaterie de l'Île d'Orléans** (p147), a short drive from Québec City.

Best for Free

Watch documentaries and thumb through interactive exhibits in the free-to-visit lobby of **MEM** (p66), Montréal's immersive social history museum, providing a deep dive into local culture.

Reach the top of **Oratoire St-Joseph** (p120), an impressive domed basilica founded by Brother André Bessette, his heart preserved in an on-site reliquary.

Eye fossils, mummies and mammoth tusks at the **Musée Redpath** (p67), an eccentric natural history collection spread across three floors on the McGill University campus.

Take a self-guided tour through the sprawling **Assemblée nationale du Québec** (p136) to admire its Second Empire architecture and bronze statues.

Wind through the streets of **Old Québec** (p132), lined with cute shops and butter-scented cafes, to experience centuries of Canadian history on every block.

Perfect Days

It could take a lifetime to uncover Montréal and Québec City's wonders. Focus on getting straight to the best spots – a blend of art, food, history, shopping and must-do outdoor activities.

Old Port (p39), Montréal

FROM LEFT: MIRCEA COSTINA/SHUTTERSTOCK, JEFFREY WHYTE/ALAMY, DEREK ROBBINS/SHUTTERSTOCK, EARTH PIXEL LLC/ALAMY

DAY ONE

Only Have One Day?

MORNING
Grab breakfast at Old Montréal's **Olive + Gourmando** (p48) before digesting 5000 years of history at archaeological museum **Pointe-à-Callière** (p44; pictured). From here, shop along Rue St-Paul en route to the hallowed **Chapelle Notre-Dame-de-Bon-Secours** (p44).

AFTERNOON
Amble to Place d'Armes, dominated by the **Basilique Notre-Dame** (p38). After peeping its interior, search for souvenirs at **Marché Saint Laurent** (p49) and **L'Affichiste** (p49). Refuel with coffee from the dazzling **Crew Collective & Café** (p43).

EVENING
Beeline to the **Old Port** (p39) for Cirque du Soleil's summertime show or to ride **La Grande Roue**. Finish with Japanese fare at **Fleurs et Cadeaux** (p69), then dance downstairs at **Sans Soleil** (p69).

— DAY TWO — — DAY THREE —

A Weekend Trip

MORNING
Energized by coffee from **Café SAT** (p67), drop by **MEM** (p66) to learn what makes Montréalers tick. Spend the rest of the morning along Blvd St-Laurent: scope **thrift stores** (p95), admire **murals** (p92) and order **Schwartz's** (p94; pictured) smoked meat.

AFTERNOON
Trek to **Belvédère Kondiaronk** (p90) for panoramic views, then hike into Downtown and get acquainted with Québécois artists at **MBAM** (p58).

DINNER
Take the Métro to La Petite-Patrie for a foodie adventure. Start by sharing a couple plates of Thai at **Pichai** (p112) and a pizza at **Marci** (p111). Cap it off with foaming brews at **Mellön** (p113) or natural wine from **Mamie** (p113).

A Short Break

MORNING
Rev your engine with a **La Maison Smith** (p143) croissant, surrounded by Place-Royale's stone edifices, then explore Old Québec's **fortifications** (p130). Skip along **Terrasse Dufferin** (p133; pictured) for views of the turreted Château Frontenac; in winter, shriek down the terrace's toboggan ramp.

AFTERNOON
Belly up to **Le Chic Shack** (p143) for gourmet poutine, then wander **Rue du Petit-Champlain** (p134), dipping into artisan shops. Save room in your schedule for cultural exhibits at **Musée de la Civilisation** (p131).

DINNER
Tuck into Québécois comfort food at **La Bûche** (p143) then unwind at **L'Oncle Antoine** (p144), sipping maple whiskey in an 18th-century vault.

If You Have More Time

Between spring and autumn, assemble a picnic at **Marché Atwater** (p120) and cycle the Lachine canal with a detour to up-and-coming Verdun. No matter the season, hop to **Parc Jean-Drapeau** (p50) – possibly for summer's Piknic Électronik party or winter's ice skating rink.

Head to the city's east side for a day. Eat everything in **HoMa** (p73) check out the elaborate interior of **Château Dufresne** (p83) and pick one of Espace Pour la Vie's magnificent science museums – perhaps the **Insectarium** (p79), where butterflies land on outstretched arms.

Shop along Ave Mont-Royal on the edge of Plateau Mont-Royal, peppered with vintage shops, artist boutiques and cafes, before ambling into Mile End to grab bagels at **Fairmount** (p108) and **St-Viateur** (p108). Don't skimp on entertainment, either. There's hockey at **Centre Bell** (p64), indie-band jamming at **Casa del Popolo** (p109), classical music at **Place des Arts** (p64) and all-night EDM at Village club **Stereo** (p85).

Insectarium (p79), Montréal

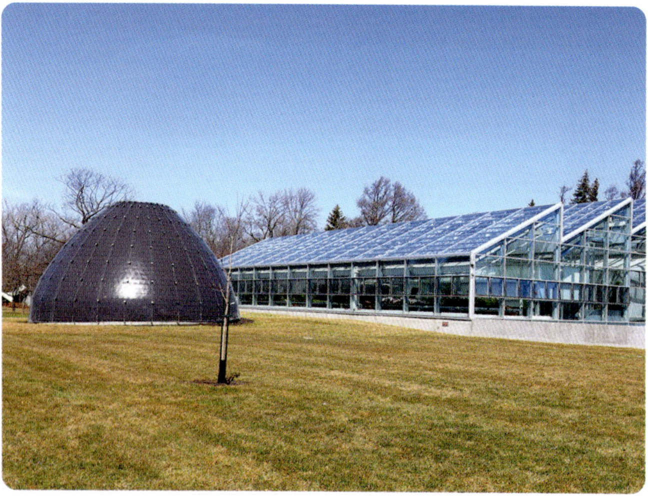

MEUNIERD/SHUTTERSTOCK

A City Day Trip

Rent a car to drive the perimeter of **Île d'Orléans** (p146), a bucolic island in the St Lawrence River. Budget for a few hours to make pit stops along the way: at 19th-century village **St-Jean**, for treats at **Chocolaterie de l'Île d'Orléans** (p147) and to taste wine from vineyards.

———

Back on the mainland, wow at the powerful falls central to **Parc de la Chute-Montmorency** (p148; pictured). Reserve two hours to wander the park's trails.

———

With more energy, drive 30 minutes to **Wendake** (p150) for dinner at **Restaurant La Traite** (p151) before walking through the **Onhwa' Lumina** (p151) arboreal light show, learning about indigenous Huron-Wendat culture.

On a Rainy Day

Bad weather is prime museum time. At Parc Olympique, spend several hours seeing at animals at the **Biodôme** (p77; pictured) and celestial films at the **Planétarium** (p78) – the complexes are connected by an underground tunnel.

———

Take the Métro Downtown to visit the social history-focused **Musée McCord Stewart** (p66) – then descend into the **Underground City** (p68), avoiding rain while walking to **Time Out Market** (p69), filled with outposts for beloved Montréal restaurants.

———

In Old Montréal, warm up with river spa **Bota Bota**'s (p46) water circuit, a preamble to cozy French food accompanied by jazz at **Modavie** (p48), followed by **Bisou Bisou**'s (p49) cocktails, refreshing as a summer's day.

Get Prepared

BOOK AHEAD

Two months before Purchase tickets for hockey games, live performances, seasonal boat tours and accommodations for major festivals.

One month before Secure reservations at trendy, high-end restaurants like Montréal's **Vin Mon Lapin** (p111) and **Alma** (p111).

One week before Check *weather.gc.aa* and pack appropriately. Download transit apps like BIXI. Consult Tourisme MTL *(mtl.org)* for special events.

Manners Matter

Kiss, kiss The two-cheek kiss – 'la bise' – is a convivial Québec greeting, not a French-kissing precursor.

Picnic law It's illegal to drink alcohol in public around Québec – unless you're at a sanctioned park space in Montréal and alcohol is accompanied by a meal.

This isn't France No need to compare Québec to its European sister nation. Locals will appreciate recognition of their distinctly Québécois culture.

Speaking French

French is Québec's official language and around 90% of locals speak it. Fluency isn't necessary – over half the population can converse in English – but knowing a little français can go a long way in showing respect. This isn't the same kind of French you'll find on Duolingo, however. Québécois French hits European ears the way a Scottish brogue hits Americans – intelligible, but occasionally confusing. Try your best.

Things to Know

Buying liquor Find reasonably-priced liquor and wine at the Société des alcools du Québec (SAQ), the province's chain of state-owned liquor stores. SAQs also sell beer, though *dépanneurs* (p28) and grocery stores carry a wider selection.

Menus Unlike English, entrée means 'appetizer' and *plat principal* means 'main course'; *dîner* means lunch and *souper* means dinner.

Winter clothing Québec can be bitterly cold from November to March or April. Follow the three-layer rule by donning a moisture-wicking base (leggings or tights), a main layer (a sweater and pants), plus an insulating jacket. Consider bringing an outer shell to protect against wind and snow. Wear sturdy boots, thick socks, warm gloves and a hat to cover the ears. There's no bad weather – only bad clothing.

TIPPING

Tipping is obligatory in restaurants, bars, taxis and hotels. Consider leaving extra money for exceptional service.

 15%
Restaurants & cocktail bars

 $1 or change
Cafes

 10–15% cash
Tour guides

 $2 per suitcase
Bellhops & porters

DAILY BUDGET

BUDGET: Less than $200

- Hostel dorm bed: **$30–80**
- Museum admission: **free–$30**
- Poutine: **$10**
- Craft beer: **$9**
- Métro ride: **$3.75**

MIDRANGE: $300–400

- B&B double room: **$150–200**
- Smoked-meat sandwich: **$15**
- History tour in Montréal or Québec City: **$50**
- Two-course dinner with wine: **$80**

TOP END: More than $500

- Boutique hotel room: **from $250**
- Ride share from Old Montréal to Mile End: **$20**
- Spa pass: **$70**
- Meal at high-end restaurant with cocktails: **$125**

Currency
Canadian dollar ($)

Languages
French, English

Time Zone
Eastern Time (GMT/UTC minus 5 hours)

HULAHOP/SHUTTERSTOCK

DISCOUNT CARD

Passeport MTL *(mtl.org/en/passeport-mtl)* provides discounts on museums, cafes and more. Buy admission for three to five major attractions and save around 35% on tickets. Check what's offered to ensure the options align with your interests.

When to Go

Winter's snowscape transforms with spring's petals and summer's dog days cool as autumn arrives. As Québec's seasons change, there's always something to celebrate.

Québec experiences four seasons in their extremes. Snow starts to appear around November and blankets the landscape until April, embraced by skaters and skiers who take to frozen ponds and parks. Spring arrives in fits and starts, sweetened by maple syrup and bursting into a floral frenzy by May. Summer is outdoor-festival season, when bikes zip along cycling trails and crowds catch rays along the St Lawrence River and outdoor terraces. Autumn becomes an arboreal art show, best appreciated in parks.

The Big Events

February: The world's largest winter festival, **Carnaval de Québec** (p138), transforms Québec City into a frosted fun zone with two weeks of sleigh rides, night parades, maple taffy and 'snow baths.'

June–July: Hear legends and newcomers improvise riffs and trills at hundreds of concerts held during the **Festival international de Jazz de Montréal** (p64).

August: The rainbow carpet is rolled out for **Fierté Montréal**, the francophone world's biggest LGBTIQ+ gathering – an 11-day fête climaxing in a celebratory parade.

August: Powerhouse performers take to stages around Parc Jean-Drapeau for **Osheaga** (p50; *osheaga.com*) a three-day music jamboree featuring everyone from emerging artists to established stars.

Montréal

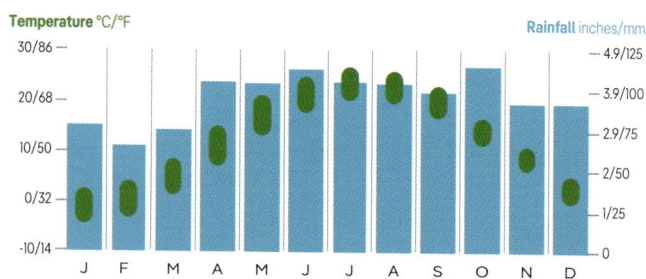

Fierté Montréal

Wacky & Wonderful Festivals

January–February (Montréal) and March (Québec City): EDM-heads don their favorite retro snowsuits for **Igloofest** (p40), staying warm by step touching under the moon as DJs spin tunes.

June: Choose between sounds of free jazz, avant folk and more experimental genres at Montréal's three-week, 50-concert **Suoni Per Il Popolo** (p109) music fest, highlighting emerging artists.

June: Blvd St-Laurent transforms into an open-air art gallery during **MURAL Festival**, when renowned street artists paint murals across Plateau Mont-Royal, accompanied by block parties featuring digital installations and live performances.

July: Just for Laughs (p65) offers two weeks of nonstop jokes, flung at crowds by stand-up greats like past performers Ali Wong, Hasan Minhaj and Margaret Cho.

--- **ACCOMMODATIONS LOWDOWN** ---

As temperatures drop, so do hotel prices, making early January and late February a fantastic time for bargains. In Montréal, short-term home rentals only operate legally between June 10 and September 10. A small portion of Rues Ste-Catherine and St-Denis offer short-term rentals year-round.

Getting There

Most visitors fly in via either Aéroport International Montréal-Trudeau (YUL) or Québec City's Aéroport international Jean-Lesage de Québec (YQB). It's also possible to arrive via bus, train or car.

From the Airport to the City Center

By Taxi or Rideshare
Fixed rates from the airport to the city center apply for both cities. **YUL** to Downtown Montréal costs $49.45 (5am to 11pm) and $56.70 (11pm to 5am). Budget for at least 25 minutes. Taxis from Québec City's YQB to Old Québec cost $41.40 during the day and $47.60 at night. Budget for 30 minutes. Rideshare app **Uber** works in both destinations.

By Bus
Purchase fares for the **'747' YUL** shuttle to Downtown Montréal with exact change on the bus or at one of the vending machines near door 28 in the international arrivals area. The standard $11 fare works as a 24-hour transit pass to ride the bus and Métro throughout Montréal. Budget for 45 minutes. At Québec City's YQB, purchase $3.75 bus tickets for the **Réseau de transport de la Capitale** (RTC) at the vending machine by the check-in counters in the terminal building. Budget for an hour.

By Train
By 2027 Montréal's **REM** (Réseau express métropolitain) train is expected to link YUL to Downtown Montréal's Gare Centrale on a 25-minute ride. Keep a lookout.

Other Points of Entry

Gare Central (Montréal)
Canada's **VIA Rail** *(viarail.ca)* connects this downtown train station to over 400 destinations across the country, including Québec City's Gare de Palais (3½ hours away). A trip along **Amtrak**'s Adirondack line *(amtrak.com)* links to NYC (10 hours away). Trains pulling into Montréal have handy Métro access to elsewhere in town.

Gare de Palais (Québec City)
This French château-inspired train-and-bus station from 1915 is within walking distance of Old Québec.

Getting Around

Québec's public transportation showcases the dynamism of its cities. Cycling lanes roll through bustling neighborhoods, ferries cruise along the St Lawrence and Montréal's Métro snakes beneath its streets. Most revealing is the pedestrian choreography of Montréal's sidewalks and Québec City's staircases, where everyone joins the dance – unless opting for a taxi, readily available.

Métro

Montréal's underground Métro system (5:30am-1am Sun-Fri, until 1:30am Sat) includes 68 stations spread across four color-coded lines covering 69km of track. It's fast, efficient and easy to navigate. Though service is less comprehensive than the bus, it's preferable, particularly while traveling around the city's downtown core.

Walking

Québec's primary cities sport historic districts chockablock with architecture that inspires slow strolling. Just don't get too caught up in details. Sidewalks are like mini highways: traffic keeps right, stopping short causes collisions, and if you want to pause for a picture, step out of the way.

Bus

Montréal's STM bus system is comprehensive but service can be slow and unpredictable. It's ideal

FROM LEFT: PORNPRASIT PANADA/SHUTTERSTOCK, CITYMAPPER APP, DEREK ROBBINS/SHUTTERSTOCK

ESSENTIAL APP
Google Maps for navigation? Sure, but **Citymapper** is more comprehensive, with trip planning details for more transportation options.
---

for reaching places disconnected from the Métro and preferable for travelers with mobility impairments. The RTC bus system is Québec City's primary public transport option, connecting downtown to the suburbs.

Taxis & Rideshares
It's easy to flag down taxis, but if you prefer to order a car via smartphone, try Uber. Montréal's Téo Taxi *(teo.taxi)* operates a lot like Uber, except its fleet of vehicles are 100% electric. Québec City's Taxi Coop *(taxiscoop-quebec.com)* is similar, though you can pay drivers in cash.

Bicycle
Montréal offers over 1000km of interconnected bike paths and nearly 200km of traffic-separated lanes. Flying through town by pedal power is fantastic for seeing the sights quickly. It's also easy, thanks to BIXI – Montréal's year-round bike-share program, with over 900 stations throughout the city.

Québec City has plans to build a 150km network of bike lanes by 2035 – though current offerings are best for leisurely pedaling along the St Lawrence. Bike-share program àVélo offers electrically-assisted bikes at 165 stations between May 1 and November 15.

Public Transport Essentials

Transit Fare
Fares for Montréal's integrated bus-and-Métro system (STM) cost the same for both modes. They're available for purchase at Métro station kiosks. For the bus, you can pay with exact change or a pre-purchased ticket. Children 11 and under ride for free. Québec City's buses also require exact change.

Bus & Métro Discounts
For extended stays in Montréal and Québec City, purchase an OPUS card ($6; pictured right) – a reusable smart card to which can be added discounted rates for bus and Métro fares. The cards are rechargeable: in Montréal, download the Chrono app *(artm.quebec/en/chrono-mobile-application)*, choose a fare type, then tap your card to your smartphone to refill. Québec City uses the RTC Nomade paiement app *(rtcquebec.ca)*. Cards can be purchased at Montréal's Métro kiosks and Québec City's RTC info centers.

Options for Montréal's discount pass include unlimited evening ($6.25; 6pm to 5am), 24 hours ($11), three days ($21.25) and 10 rides ($33.25). Québec City's pass options are one day ($10), unlimited weekend ($17.50), five consecutive days ($33.25) and bundles of 20 rides ($63).

Bike-share Fares
If you're only planning to hop on a Montréal BIXI bike several times, opt for single rides ($1.50 to unlock; 20¢ per minute on a manual bike). Serious cyclists save by purchasing a monthly membership ($23; additional costs for rides over 45 minutes). Download the BIXI app to pay and unlock bikes. Québec City's electric àVélo offers single rides ($1 to unlock; 33¢ per minute), 24-hour multi-trip passes ($19; additional costs for rides over 45 minutes), plus month passes. Both BIXI and àVélo charge a $100 security deposit.

TRAVEL COSTS

Montréal Métro
$3.75

Québec City buses
$3.75

10-minute bike-share MTL/QC
$3.50/4.30

PAY THE FARE

Fare evasion on Montréal's Métro can result in fines ranging from $150 to $500.

ACCESSIBLE TRANSIT
Plan trips around Montréal using the STM route planner *(stm.info)*; click the 'wheelchair accessible' option. Most STM buses can lower their floors to sidewalk level and extend ramps for wheelchairs. Only 30 of Montréal's Métro stations have elevators. Québec City's bus routes offer ramp-equipped vehicles, and it's possible to request wheelchair-accessible ride share services through Uber WAV and Taxi Lévis *(taxilevis.ca)*. Avoid Old Québec's steep steps by riding the funicular between Terrasse Dufferin and Rue du Petit-Champlain.

SHAWN.CCF/SHUTTERSTOCK

A Few Surprises

Syrup, staircases and Québécois French all make Québec special – it's no wonder this province tried seceding from Canada.

Sacred Swear Words

Tabernacle. Chalice. Sacrament. Host. In English these words might evoke images of holy choirs and communion cups, but yell them in Québécois French and you're spewing some of the province's dirtiest profanities. These are *sacres* – Québec's signature swear words, which take aim at one of its defining institutions. While the naughtiest English-language swear words often focus on terms and taboos related to sex and bodily functions, Québec's foulest language stems from its Catholic upbringing. Linguistic historians say this sacred swearing developed in the 19th century as a rebellious pushback against religious control. As Catholic fervor fades, some wonder how long these slurs will survive. For now, however, they're part of local parlance – so think twice before yelling 'Tabarnak!' in a crowd. It might not go over well.

Neighborhood Dépanneurs

They may look like convenience stores or delis – but in Québec, they're called *dépanneurs* and are a provincial institution. Derived from the French verb 'to help out', 'deps' (the abbreviation) are neighborhood lifelines for groceries, cleaning supplies, snacks and three beloved vices: beer, cigarettes and lotto tickets. They first popped up in Montréal in 1970, capitalizing on a legal loophole: small merchants with no more than two employees could stay open on nights and weekends, continuing to sell goods when other stores closed. Over 1000 deps dot Montréal today, each with a personality reflecting the metropolitan mosaic. Some are no-frills, carrying only the basics, while others specialize in Japanese sushi rolls or Egyptian street sandwiches, highlighting each owner's immigrant origins. **Le Petit Dep**, a chain with Montréal (p49) and Québec City (p144) locations, doubles as a cafe, where you can lounge with a latte after perusing a selection of kitchen staples and Québec-themed souvenirs.

Confusing Cardinal Directions

In Montréal, what's called 'north' on street signs is really northwest, 'south' is often east. Blame 17th-century colonists for this compass confusion. When the French laid out their settlement's street grid, they treated the St Lawrence River as its guiding star. Streets running parallel to the river were labeled 'west' and 'east', and anything perpendicular became 'north' and 'south.' They weren't entirely wrong. The St Lawrence technically flows west to east from Lake Ontario to the Atlantic Ocean, but it swerves northward around Montréal, making the original French design slightly off-kilter. The result? A city built around geocentric river logic instead of cardinal directions – and, as some like to say, 'the only city where the sun sets in the north.'

Maple Syrup

Maple syrup is a Québec tradition started by Indigenous communities, picked up by French colonizers and now a cultural cornerstone. More than 5000 maple farms practice the ancient alchemy of transforming sap into sugar during the short 'sugaring off' season between February and March, when sap flows from trees. The province produces around 70% of the world's supply, and this liquid gold contributes $1.1 billion to Canada's economy. Due to the product's dependence on erratic and ever-changing weather, Québec stockpiles the world's only reserve of maple syrup. Three warehouses hold the equivalent of 52

Maple-syrup taffy

Ruelle verte

Olympic-size syrup pools, ensuring waffles worldwide never go dry, no matter the success of a harvest. Québécois take serious pride in all things maple – most evident from March through April, when they head to countryside *cabanes à sucres* (sugar shacks) to celebrate the season's bounty with sugar-soaked food fests. But there's no need to wait for spring to indulge. In Québec, maple syrup gets turned into candies, mixed into sauces, used to glaze meats, and dripped into coffee and cocktails.

Iconic Staircases

Twirling outdoor staircases are an architectural element synonymous with Montréal. Common in neighborhoods like the Plateau, Mile End and Villeray, these features date to the mid-19th century, when a population boom led to strong housing demand. The solution? Multiplexes: residential buildings with units stacked atop one another. To maximize interior space while conforming to rules, new constructions got creative and placed upper-unit stairs outside. Though these were baned in the 1940s, Montréalers reignited their corkscrew-step romance in the 1970s. They might be harrowing in ice storms and horrible on moving day, but when you look down a street of spiraling iron, it's easy to see why they're beloved.

Québec City is also known for staircases – but unlike Montréal's residential runners, these flights act as public arteries, connecting Old Québec's Upper Town and Lower Town. Nearly 30 sets of stairs decorate the streetscape. The first, **Escalier Casse-Cou** (p134), was built in 1635; the longest, Cap-Blanc, covers 398 steps with platforms where pedestrians can pause to catch their breath.

Flurry of Festivals

Québec hosts more than 500 celebrations throughout the year – and Montréal reigns as queen of the party scene. Place des Festivals, a pedestrian square in the city's downtown core, is tailor-made for these fêtes, where hundreds of thousands of spectators gather for events like **Festival international de Jazz de Montréal** (p64). If you can think it, there's a chance the city has a festival for it: poutine, poetry, mixology, science, street art, street food, fireworks, race cars – and that's just the short list. Festival frenzy burns hottest in summer. It's wise to check what's scheduled before planning a trip; Tourisme Montréal (*mtl.org*) is a fantastic resource. There are plenty of public parties in wintertime, too, including the world's biggest **winter carnival** (p138), hosted in Québec City.

Ruelles Vertes

Hundreds of Montréal's back alleys serve as community corridors called *ruelles vertes* (green alleys). The city officially recognizes more than 450 of these linear laneways, providing front-row seats to the backstage lives of locals. You might run into flower-filled gardens, weekend block parties, outdoor dinner hangs or an occasional impromptu concert. Some sport eye-catching murals. In Plateau Mont-Royal you can walk south to north almost entirely along these peaceful paths, many of which come alive in early summer evenings. Find your way by consulting the map on *ruellesvertes demontreal.ca*.

OFFBEAT MONTRÉAL & QUÉBEC CITY

- Fall in love with Montréal's quirky cabaret artists, be it drag maven **Cabaret Mado** (p82) or the burlesque beauties of **Wiggle Room** (p96).
- Pedal to **Île de la Visitation** (p104), a tree-lined island connected to industrial ruins along Rivière des Prairies – Montréal's other river.
- Go on a food crawl through up-and-coming neighborhood **Hochelaga-Maisonneuve** (p83) sampling chocolates, cheeses and beer.
- Tour the **Morrin Centre** (p142), Québec City's only dedicated English library, with a graffiti-etched crypt recalling its 19th-century prison days.
- See a gallery of 'bad art' at **EXMURO** (p140), a contemporary art hub in Québec City paying homage to artists who tried their best and failed.

Explore Montréal & Québec City

Old Montréal	35
Downtown & Chinatown	55
Quartier Latin, the Village & HoMa	73
Plateau Mont-Royal	87
Mile End, Little Italy & Outremont	101
Lachine Canal & Southwest Montréal	115
Québec City	127

Worth a Trip

Île d'Orléans	146
Parc de la Chute-Montmorency	148
Wendake	150

Montréal & Québec City's Walking & Cycling Tours

Eavesdrop on Old Grudges	42
Stroll the Golden Square Mile	60
Sample Chinatown's Cuisine	62
Saunter Through the Gayborhood	80
See Magnificent Murals	92
Jump into Jewish History	106
Cycle the Lachine Canal	118
Stroll Through Old Québec	132

Parc du Mont-Royal (p90), Montréal
SHAWN.CCF/SHUTTERSTOCK

Explore
Old Montréal

Researched by John Garry

Montréal's story starts here – amid crooked alleyways and lively plazas of the city's oldest streets. Founded as the devout Catholic colony Ville-Marie in 1642, Vieux-Montréal (Old Montréal) quickly became an important fur-trading outpost for New France before ceding to British control in the 1760s. While its facades whisper of 18th-century nuns, 19th-century bankers and 20th-century industrialization, its shops, restaurants and recreational spaces tell another tale – of a trendsetting city adept at reinvention. Spin around architecturally alluring Place d'Armes, shop down action-packed Rue St-Paul then hop on a boat at the Old Port to admire the St Lawrence River, the waterway that made Montréal.

Getting Around

 Métro
Take the orange line to Square-Victoria (west), Place-d'Armes (central) or Champ-de-Mars (east) and walk south into Old Montréal.

 Bus
Bus 14 runs along Rue Notre-Dame in Old Montréal between Rue Berri and Blvd St-Laurent. Bus 55 stops along Blvd St-Laurent. Bus 50 runs along Rue de la Commune by the Old Port.

 **Walk & Bicycle**
Most major sights, shops and restaurants line walkable Rues St-Paul and Notre-Dame. A cycling path connects the Old Port to Lachine Canal and beyond.

THE BEST

ARCHAEOLOGICAL LEGACY
Pointe-à-Callière (p44)

GOTHIC REVIVAL CHURCH
Basilique Notre-Dame (p38)

ECO-FRIENDLY BOAT
Petit Navire (p46)

RIVERSIDE SPA
Bota Bota (p46)

CONTEMPORARY ART
Fonderie Darling (p46)

Old Port (p39)
SUSANNE POMMER/SHUTTERSTOCK

OLD MONTRÉAL

Square-Victoria
Ave Viger Ouest
Rue St-Alexandre
Ave Viger Ouest
Place-d'Armes
Palais des Congrès
Rue St-Urbain
Autoroute Ville-Marie
18
Rue St-Antoine Ouest
Sq Victoria
Rue St-Pierre
Rue St-Jacques
11
Rue St-François-Xavier
Côte de la Pl. d'Armes
27
Rue St-Jacques
Rue Square-Victoria
19
Rue Notre-Dame Ouest
20
21
26
Basilique Notre-Dame
Rue Notre-Dame Ouest
Rue Ste-Hélène
Rue de l'Hôpital
13
OLD MONTRÉAL
Le Petit Dep
Rue St-Maurice
Rue de Longueuil
Rue McGill
Rue Le Moyne
12 PHI
14 24
10
16 9
Rue St-Paul Ouest
Rue St-Henri
5
15
Pl Royale
Rue St-Paul Ouest
Pl d'Youville
Pl d'Youville
1
Pointe-à-Callière
Rue William
Rue de la Commune Ouest
Fonderie Darling 6
Rue St-Normand
Rue St-Pierre
28
Grand Quai
Rue Ottawa
Rue Marguerite d'Youville
Rue Wellington
Promenade du Vieux-Port
Rue des Sœurs-Grises
Rue McGill
Rue King
Bota Bota
8
Bassin Alexandra
Rue Prince
Rue Queen
Rue de la Commune Ouest
Parc des Écluses

For more see
- ⭐ Top Experiences p38
- ✳ Experiences p44
- ✖ Eating p48
- 🅳 Drinking p49
- 🛍 Shopping p49

Rue Mill
Silo No 5

Basilique Notre-Dame

Montréal's grande dame of Catholic churches opened in 1829 and was made a minor basilica in 1982. It's a showstopper with Gothic Revival twin towers soaring 69m high and a midnight-blue ceiling glittering with 24-karat gold stars.

MAP P36 **D2**

PLANNING TIPS

Purchase tickets for daytime sightseeing or the evening Aura Experience: doing both is overkill. Download the informational pamphlet from *basiliquenotredame.ca* for insight about the church's artwork.

Amazing Interior

Inside the main hall, look for the 7000-pipe **Casavant Frères organ** and the swirling staircase leading to the **Pulpit of Truth**, with prophets Ezekiel and Jeremiah crouched at its base. This hand-carved forest of ornate wooden pillars was constructed without a single nail. Venture beyond the main hall to admire the 20-ton bronze altarpiece in the **Notre-Dame-du-Sacré-Coeur Chapel**. Panels throughout the church provide backstories on the art.

The Aura Experience

For a psychedelic encounter with the divine, plan a trip around the **Aura Experience**, a 25-minute cinematically soundtracked light show highlighting the basilica's elegant architecture in three distinct acts. Arrive 15 to 30 minutes before showtime to wander around the illuminated stations – and don't miss the trippy portrait of Marguerite Bourgeoys glowing on the altar's left-hand side. For the perfect seat, aim for three or four pillars back from the main pulpit to take it all in.

Catholic Convert

Notre-Dame's New York–based architect, Irish Protestant James O'Donnell, converted to Catholicism before dying in 1930, ensuring his final resting place could be the church crypt.

Scan this QR code for opening hours and tickets.

⭐ TOP EXPERIENCE

Old Port

Montréal's historic center for maritime trade, the **Old Port** *(Vieux-Port de Montréal; oldportofmontreal.com)*, is now a recreational fun zone stretching along a 2km promenade paralleling the St Lawrence River. Explore its four major quais (quays) for a host of family-oriented adventures and festivals.

MAP P37 **G3**

Quai de l'Horloge

The Old Port's **easternmost quay** is a summertime sensation thanks to **Plage de l'Horloge** (Clock Tower Beach), an urban sand patch open June to September that's dotted with sea-blue umbrellas, lounge chairs and misting stations (swimming isn't allowed). Grab a drink from the on-site bistro (serving slushies, wine and water) and enjoy views of the St Lawrence flowing beneath Pont Jacques-Cartier. Admission is free outside ticketed events, such as evening DJ sets for 18-and-over crowds. It's a fantastic spot to watch fireworks erupt over the river during **l'International des Feux Loto-Québec**. The scene is anchored by the cream-white, 45m-high beaux-arts **Tour de l'Horloge**, constructed in 1922 to honor sailors lost in WWI.

PLANNING TIP
In summer, head to Quai Jacques-Cartier for river tours and to ride the river shuttle *(navettes fluviales.com)* to Parc Jean-Drapeau.

La Grande Roue de Montréal

Walkways from the Promenade du Vieux-Port and Quai de l'Horloge lead to **Parc du Bassin Bonsecours**, dominated by **La Grande Roue de Montréal** *(lagranderouedemontreal.com; adult/child $27.50/15)*. This is Canada's tallest observation wheel, with 42 roomy gondolas that whisk riders 60m into the air for 360-degree views. With temperature-controlled cabins, leather seats and

Scan the QR code for info on hours and upcoming events.

BENJAMIN MALKA/SHUTTERSTOCK

TAKE A BREAK
Stands along the Promenade du Vieux-Port sell street-style eats in summer; most offerings tend toward mediocrity. Find tastier fare on Rue St-Paul, like **Stash Café**, close to the Grand Quai.

a smooth ride, it's the Cadillac of Ferris wheels, open year-round. Expect long summer lines; beat the ticket queue by purchasing online in advance.

Quai Jacques-Cartier & Quai King Edward

Most people stop by **Quai Jacques-Cartier** between spring and summer to see acrobats fly under the Big Top with **Cirque du Soleil** (pictured; *cirquedusoleil.com; from $83*), one of the city's most famous exports. These gravity-defying shows rarely disappoint – don't pass up a chance to see a home-turf performance.

Come mid-January, crowds return for alfresco fête **Igloofest** *(igloofest.ca)*, a four-week outdoor electronic music festival where people bundle up in vintage ski suits to dance under the stars. Grooving to a lineup of renowned DJs is the fantastic way to heat up Montréal's coldest months.

Quai King Edward

Moving west, along **Quai King Edward** you'll find **Centre des Sciences de Montréal** *(centredessciencesdemontreal.com; adult/child $28/18.50)*. Hands-on exhibits appeal to budding scientists, tech tots and anyone young at heart. There's also an immersive **IMAX movie theater** playing science-themed films on a seven-story screen. Accessibility is a cornerstone of the museum, making this a fantastic option for folks with limited mobility or developmental disabilities.

Grand Quai

The **Grand Quai** is like the Old Port's greatest hits on one 305m-long dock. Step inside the Port Center to explore a free, interactive, kid-friendly exhibit on Montréal's role in the global supply chain. Catch rays on the 2nd-story green roof, with 24,000 flowering plants blooming around the terrace. The **Port of Montréal Tower** *(port-montreal.com; adult/child $15/10)* is a 65m-high observatory with hands-on displays, panoramic views and a glassed-in cage where visitors can see straight down to the docks below. It's open June to September and one week around Christmas and spring break.

Thrills for All Ages

Dive off a 64m platform at **Montréal Bungee** *(montrealbungee.com; Mar-Dec; from $179)* – Canada's highest bungee jump – on Quai des Convoyeurs. The child-friendly **Tyrolienne MTL Zipline** *(mtlzipline.com; May-Sep; adult/child $20/17)* is a 25m-high, 365m-long thrill ride over Bassin Bonsecours. Kids go bananas for ropes courses around pirate-themed adventure park **Voiles en Voiles** *(voilesenvoiles.com; Apr-Oct; from $29)*.

INDUSTRIAL ARCHITECTURE

Look west past Bota Bota to see **Silo No 5.** Constructed in four stages from 1906 and 1958, the 500m-long, 66.4m-high behemoth shot into the sky as Montréal became the world's largest grain port. Shuttered in 1994, it's now the only ghostly remnant of the port's era as a global grain hub.

WALKING TOUR

Eavesdrop on Old Grudges

Old Montréal's streets were where French colonists vied for supremacy against Indigenous communities and British forces imposed control over francophone pioneers. Though the fighting ended long ago, monuments, plazas and facades throughout the 'hood whisper of centuries-old grievances.

START	END	LENGTH
Place Jacques-Cartier	Place de la Grande-Paix-de-Montréal	1.5km; 45 mins

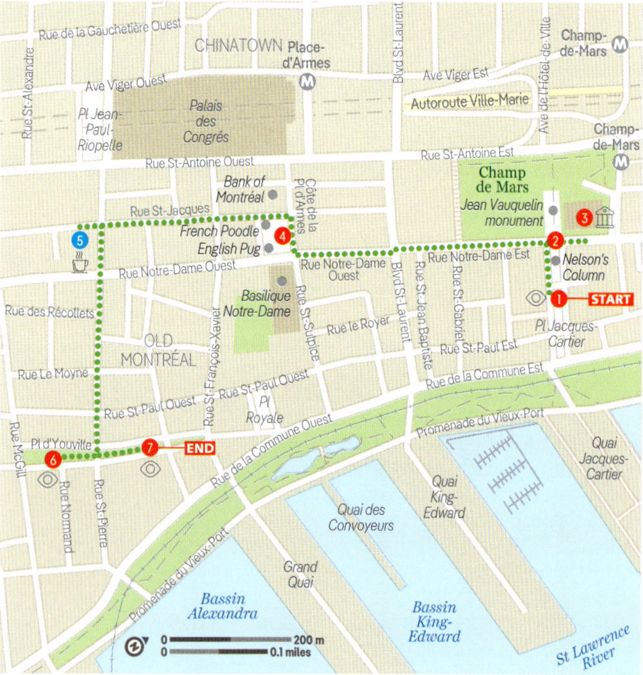

1 Original Explorers

Start at the center of **Place Jacques-Cartier**, named for the French explorer who claimed Canada for France in 1535, despite the fact that Indigenous communities had been here for thousands of years. At the plaza's center sits a *cabane à sucre* (sugar shack); grab a maple candy for the journey.

2 Foreign Foes

Stand along **Rue Notre-Dame** to witness a statues embodying centuries of Anglo-Franco feuding. Nelson's Column is topped by British Admiral Horatio Nelson, who died defeating the French at the Battle of Trafalgar. He gazes north (going by street sign logic; see p28) toward a monument honoring French naval officer Jean Vauquelin, who fought British forces during the French and Indian War.

3 Freedom of Speech

The balcony of **Hôtel de Ville** (City Hall) is where French President Charles de Gaulle ended a 1967 speech with 'Vive le Québec libre!' ('Long live free Québec!') – a rallying cry for Québec separatists who desired independence from Canada. His exclamation emboldened the province's French-speaking sovereignty movement.

4 Cultural Differences

Look west at **Place d'Armes** to spot two snooty statues: The English Pug and the French Poodle (2013). An English pug owner judges the French-Catholic **Basilique Notre-Dame**; his French counterpart glares at the British-influenced Bank of Montréal. Step inside the Bank of Montréal to see its 20m-tall coffered ceiling.

5 Coffee Break

Follow Rue St-Jacques, dubbed Canada's Wall St, to witness the fight for seats waged at **Crew Collective & Café** *(crewcollectivecafe.com; 8am-4pm)* – Montréal's most beautiful coffee shop. Wow over the ornate interior, constructed for the Royal Bank of Canada in the 1920s.

6 Pyrotechnic Parliament

Stand atop **Place d'Youville**. This location was briefly the capital seat of the Province of Canada until outraged anglophones torched the Parliament building in 1849, following the passage of a bill favorable to French Canadians.

7 Struggle for Peace

End at **Place de la Grande-Paix-de-Montréal**, where 39 Indigenous communities agreed to peace with New France in 1701. Peace unraveled with the British conquest of 1760. The fight for Indigenous rights continues.

EXPERIENCES

Dig into History at Musée Pointe-à-Callière
ARCHAEOLOGY MUSEUM

MAP: ❶ P36 **D3**

This is where Montréal was born – above remnants of Fort Ville-Marie, the city's first French settlement, and on grounds occupied by Indigenous Peoples for thousands of years. The fascinating, informative **Pointe-à-Callière** *(pacmusee.qc.ca; adult $29)* invites visitors to explore an underground labyrinth connecting six pavilions covering roughly 5000 years of local history. It's a fantastic first stop in the city, providing context for the making of Montréal. Budget for a couple of hours and it's closed Mondays.

Begin with **Crossroads Montréal**, an exhibit exploring the region's Indigenous underpinnings and growth as a commerce hub. Next, stroll through the city's first collector sewer to see **Where Montréal Began** – on the actual site where Paul de Chomedey de Maisonneuve and Jeanne Mance founded Ville-Marie in 1642. Continue with **Building Montréal**, featuring an informative mini-film chronicling the spread of human activity on the island.

Several engaging interactive exhibits appeal to kids; second-floor restaurant **Bistro L'Arrivage** provides St Lawrence River views. Continue to the 3rd-floor belvedere for an Old Port panorama.

Look up at Chapelle Notre-Dame-de-Bon-Secours
CHURCH AND MUSEUM

MAP: ❷ P37 **H2**

The enchanting **Chapelle Notre-Dame-de-Bon-Secours** from 1771 *(margueritebourgeoys.org; church free, museum adult/child $14/5)* is chock-full of charm. Gaze toward the vaulted ceiling to see model-boat votives floating above. In the late 18th century, the church became a place of pilgrimage for people who survived the arduous

---

 FROM MISSION TO METROPOLIS

Religion was Montréal's original raison d'être. In 1642 a band of French Catholic colonizers landed on the banks of the St Lawrence with the intention of 'saving' the Indigenous population by converting them to Catholicism. Paul de Chomedey, Sieur de Maisonneuve, a 30-year-old nobleman-turned-governor, led the missionaries alongside Jeanne Mance, a 35-year-old nurse. They dubbed their settlement Ville-Marie (City of Mary) – honoring the Holy Virgin – and set to work, clinging to faith despite disease, starvation and Iroquois attacks. By 1650 the settlement's purpose flipped from Holy Father fervor to fur trading, and in 1705 'Ville-Marie' became 'Montréal.'

Atlantic crossing. Sailors gifted the church votives as gratitude for their successful voyage, and in the 19th century, a statue of the Virgin Mary as 'Star of the Sea' was added atop the chapel's river-facing belvedere. Leonard Cohen fans will recognize her as 'our Lady of the Harbor,' featured in his lilting song *Suzanne*.

This church stands today thanks to Marguerite Bourgeoys (1620—1700) – New France's first teacher and Canada's first female saint. She launched the chapel's initial construction in 1655. The attached **museum** tells Bourgeoys' story. Descend into the chapel crypt to see artifacts spanning thousands of years of local history before climbing into the bell tower for Old Port views.

Visit Château Ramezay HOUSE MUSEUM
MAP: 3 P37 G2

Skip through 500 years of Montréal history inside **Château Ramezay** *(chateauramezay.qc.ca; adult/child $14.50/6)*, a three-story manor built in 1705. The French-style home came at a hefty cost for former Montréal governor Claude de Ramezay, who went into debt financing its steeply pitched roof and stately fieldstone walls – a bold design, considering his neighbors primarily lived in wooden houses at the time. These days it houses a small museum recounting local history from Indigenous settlement through the 20th century, with 30,000 objects in its permanent collection. Costumed guides offer tours, included with entry (daily in summer; weekends in winter). Their New France–style garb might come off as cheesy theatricality, but the knowledgeable staff impart valuable insight. Even if you don't go inside, plan to visit the manor's formal French garden, planted with vegetables, medicinal herbs and ornamental flowers. It's free and open to visitors from spring through autumn.

Step into Lieu Historique de Sir George-Étienne Cartier DESIGN AND POLITICS
MAP: 4 P37 H2

Architectural heritage and political history make fascinating bedfellows at **Lieu Historique de Sir George-Étienne Cartier** *(parkscanada.gc.ca/cartier; adult/child $4.50/free)*. The National Historic Site, open to the public on select days from mid-June to mid-December, consists of two historic houses owned by Cartier (1814—1873) – a politician who lobbied to unite Canada and was posthumously dubbed Father of the Confederation. Exhibitions in the first home explore Cartier's life and career; the second is a meticulous restoration of his Victorian abode, dripping in 1860s design. It's lovely around Christmas, decked out for a 19th-century bourgeois celebration.

Immerse Yourself in Culture at PHI & Fonderie Darling
CONTEMPORARY ART CRAWL

Head west of Blvd St-Laurent to trade Rue St-Paul's conventional galleries for experimental art. First up is **PHI** (MAP: 5 P36 C3; *phi.ca; hours vary*), celebrating the intersection of art, design and technology in three Old Montréal buildings with galleries, live performance spaces and a cinema. Many exhibits lean immersive. Admission to the 451 and 465 Rue St-Jeanne spaces is free. For film screenings at 407 Rue St-Pierre, see what's playing and reserve tickets in advance *(suggested $20 donation)*. The organization plans to unify its spaces under one roof by 2028; check the site for updates on this.

Head further west for **Fonderie Darling** (MAP: 6 P36 A4; *fonderiedarling.org; $8*), a cavernous two-room gallery in what was a 19th-century metal foundry. Scope the calendar for openings, when you can peek inside the upstairs studios of 12 artists in residence. On Thursdays from June to August between 5pm and 10pm, performance artists take over the stone patio near the entrance. Scan the schedule to see what's on; outdoor performances are free and it's closed Mondays and Tuesdays.

Hop Aboard Le Petit Navire
ECO-FRIENDLY BOATING

MAP: 7 P37 F3

Get acquainted with Montréal's *fleuve* (river that flows into the sea) on a seasonal boat tour departing from the Old Port. You can get drenched to the bone on a jet-boat trip organised by **Saute-Moutons** *(jetboatingmontreal.com)* or take it slow while dining on a 750-passenger **Croisières AML ship** *(croisieresaml.com)*.

If you'd rather experience the water sans noisy motor or cruise-style crowds, opt for a ride with **Petit Navire** *(lepetitnavire.ca)*. From mid-May to mid-October, the company's carbon-neutral fleet – all Japanese lifeboats repurposed as quiet electric vessels – takes groups of 20 to 30 people on intimate sailing adventures to Montréal's coastal treasures. Most popular is the 45-minute **Old Port of Montréal Tour** *(adult/child $30/14)*, which departs from Quai Jacques-Cartier (p40) to the Lachine Canal before looping back along the Old Port. Guests can order drinks (beer, wine and water) while the captain provides a historical deep dive.

Soak it All Up at Bota Bota
RIVERSIDE SPA

MAP: 8 P36 C5

Melt into the mighty St Lawrence at **Bota Bota** *(botabota.ca, starting at $75)*, the floating Finnish spa steaming along the Old Port piers at Rue McGill. Water is in the DNA of this four-floor pleasure palace. Originally built as a ferry in the 1950s, it was revamped in 2010 with saunas, steam rooms, heated pools, cold plunges and meditation rooms where visitors can unwind while ogling views of the city skyline and Silo No 5 (p41). The basic Water Circuit package includes access to the spa's top two floors and an outdoor garden. Massages, facials and food cost extra – unnecessary to reap Bota Bota's body-high benefits.

Bota Bota is open year-round, though it's particularly magical in winter, when you can soak in alfresco hot tubs, dispelling winter's chill above the frozen St Lawrence. Bring a bathing suit, a pair of flip-flops and a water bottle. Bota Bota provides towels and bathrobes.

Shop Along Rue St-Paul Ouest   MONTRÉAL'S OLDEST STREET

Walk along **Rue St-Paul Ouest** (MAP: 9 P36 D3) – first paved with cobblestone in the 1670s – and you might forget you're in North America. With sounds of *bonjour* pouring out doors of 19th-century buildings, this is as close as you'll get to a historic French village without crossing the Atlantic. This strip of Rue St-Paul covers roughly 1.2km. Budget a couple of hours for leisurely shopping.

Start by admiring the metal dome crowning **Marché Bonsecours** (*marchebonsecours.qc.ca*), a neoclassical structure from the 1840s. The building has been everything from a farmers market to a concert venue – and it even served briefly as Montréal's city hall (1852–78). These days it houses tourist-targeted shops; the architecture eclipses the indoor offerings.

Continue west through Place Jacques-Cartier (p43) to find more souvenirs, art galleries and coffee shops. Search **L'Empreinte Coopérative** (*lempreintecoop.com*) for Québec-made crafts, admire canvases created by local street artists at **L'Original** (*loriginal.org*) and stop inside **Le Petit Dep** (MAP: P36 D3) for a snack.

🌊 HIGHWAY H2O

The St Lawrence River is Montréal's lifeline, a 1200km highway from Lake Ontario to the Atlantic, linking Europe to North America's interior. It's how the city's major players arrived, from explorer Jacques Cartier to successive waves of immigrants. The river sparked battles, powered a 19th-century industrial boom and still fuels commerce today: 39 million tons of goods move through Montréal annually, making it Canada's second-busiest port. It's a migratory superhighway too, attracting 400 bird species, and more than 80 land and aquatic mammals. The river is also a source of sustenance: when you drink from the tap, you're tasting the St Lawrence (filtered, thankfully).

LISTINGS

Best Places for...

$ Budget $$ Midrange $$$ Top End

See p36 for map of locations

Eating

Breakfast & Brunch

Dandy $$
⑪ C2
Comfy banquettes buzz with hungry hordes helping themselves to ricotta pancakes, yolky breakfast bowls and boozy brunch cocktails close to Place d'Armes. *dandymtl.com, 10am-4pm*

Olive et Gourmando $$
⑫ C3
Enjoy heaping sandwiches, salads and all-day breakfast plates at this homey hang steps from the Old Port. Expect summer crowds. *oliveetgourmando.com, 8am-6pm*

Budget-friendly Lunch

Titanic $
⑬ C2
Sink into this sub-floor dining room among Old Montréal's worker bees for sandwich-style plates with Mexican and Italian influences. *titanicmontreal.com, 10:30am-4:30pm Mon-Fri*

Ciccio's $
⑭ C3
Wash down paninis, antipasti and salads with well-pulled espresso shots from this cheery 1950s-style sandwich counter. *cicciomtl.com, 9am-8pm*

Dinner on Rue St-Paul

Stash Café $$
⑮ C3
Sit in a church pew and fill up on traditional Polish comfort food such as pierogi at Stash, going strong since the 1970s. *restaurantstashcafe.ca, hours vary*

Wolf & Workman $$
⑯ D3
Dining on elevated pub grub in this 1830s stone building recalls when Britain ruled Montréal. *wolfandworkman.com, 11:30am-1am Mon-Fri, 10am-1am Sat & Sun*

Modavie $$$
⑰ E3
Live bands jazz up daily dinner and weekend brunch at this French bistro with old-world charm. *modavie.com, 11:30am-11pm Mon-Fri, from 10:30am Sat & Sun*

Upscale Dining

Toqué! $$$
⑱ B1
Go for the seven-course tasting menu at this fine-dining star, sourcing ingredients from artisan farmers since 1993. *restaurant-toque.com, 11:30am-1:45pm & 5:30-9:30pm Tue-Sat*

Monarque $$$
⑲ B2
Dine à la carte in the Brasserie or try the Salle à Manger's tasting menu at this boisterous, wine-walled restaurant on Montréal's former Wall St. *restaurantmonarque.ca, hours vary*

L'Orignal $$$
⑳ C2
Winter's antidote? Gorging on classic Québécois dishes (venison, wild boar, rabbit) in a cozy dining room. *restaurantlorignal.com, 5-10pm Wed & Thu, 5-11pm Fri & Sat*

Drinking

Cute Cafes

Tommy Café
21 C2

Sun streams through high-arched windows into this tri-level corner cafe with regal crown moulding, foaming cappuccinos, toasts and bowls. *tommycafe.ca, 8am-6pm*

Chez Mère Grand
22 H1

French owner Roman Beiso presides over this cozy cafe and kitchen serving made-from-scratch sandwiches, pastries and espresso drinks. *@cafemeregrand, 7:30am-4pm Mon-Fri, 8:30am-3pm Sat, 9am-3pm Sun*

Le Petit Dep
10 D3

Step behind the mint-green facade of this upscale *dépanneur* (convenience store) chain for artisanal treats. *lepetitdep.com, 8am-8pm Sun-Thu, to 10pm Fri, to 6pm Sat*

Bars

Bisou Bisou
23 F2

It's always summer at this low-level bar with Mediterranean island vibes pouring expertly-mixed, low-ABV apéritif cocktails. *barbisoubisou.com, 4pm-midnight Tue-Sun*

Buvette Pastek
24 C3

Swirl Old World and Québec vinos around stemmed glasses inside this oenophile outlet with light bites and once-a-month wine tastings. *buvettepastek.com, hours vary*

Coldroom
25 F3

Enter this underground lounge by ringing the doorbell reading 'Patience' – which you may need while waiting for a seat. *thecoldroommtl.com, 5pm-1am Sun-Thu, 3pm-1am Fri & Sat*

Shopping

Prints & Souvenirs

L'Affichiste
26 D2

Karen Etingin's poster gallery sells designs by local artists repping Montréal destinations along with stacks of vintage belle époque and mid-century modern ads. *laffichiste.com, 9am-5pm Thu-Mon*

Marché Saint Laurent
27 D2

Forget Rue St-Paul's chintzy souvenirs. Grab your MTL swag (prints, totes, artisanal maple syrup) from this boutique-cafe off Place d'Armes. *marchesaintlaurent.com, hours vary*

Indigenous Art

Sacred Fire Productions
28 C4

A non-profit gallery space with shows rotating every three months to highlight different Indigenous makers. A small shop sells prints, jewelry, books and more hand-crafted items. *productionsfeuxsacres.ca, hours vary*

Wachiya
29 F3

Find fur-lined mittens, bags and leather shoes stitched with geometric designs by the Eeyou Istchee's Cree community – northern Québec's largest traditional territory of the Cree people. *wachiya.com, 11am-7pm*

⭐ **TOP EXPERIENCE**

Parc Jean-Drapeau

Exhale around this park's 268 hectares, covering two St Lawrence River islands replete with outdoor activities. Île Ste-Hélène, closest to Old Montréal, went from military outpost to public park in the 19th century. Île Notre-Dame was built for Expo 67, an ambitious 20th-century fair. Budget for half a day.

GETTING THERE
Take the yellow line from Berri-UQAM to Jean-Drapeau, near the center of Île Ste-Hélène and the Biosphère. Bus 777 stops at Jean-Drapeau and Île Notre-Dame's casino.

Appreciate Futuristic Architecture

The **Biosphère** (pictured; *espacepourlavie.ca; adult/child $23.75/12.25*) is the park's visual pièce de résistance, rising above the tree line as an architectural emblem of Expo 67. American inventor Buckminster Fuller designed the geodesic dome, originally wrapped in an acrylic skin, as the festival's US pavilion. A 1976 fire destroyed the covering but left the most striking features intact: a webbed skeleton of steel tubes reaching 62m high and 76m across.

Today the dome houses one of the five science museums of **Espace pour la vie** (p76) with exhibits related to climate change, biodiversity and sustainable living. Programs generally appeal to elementary-school-aged children, with plenty of interactive activities for curious minds.

Dance Until Dusk

If you can't make it to **Osheaga** (*osheaga.com/en*), the three-day music fest that overtakes the park in August, don't worry. Summer Sundays are always a sonic celebration thanks to **Piknic Électronik** (*piknicelectronik.com; tickets from $24*), a weekly alfresco EDM fête from May to October. You can spend all day bopping between beats on two

Scan the QR code for information on park hours and events.

R.M. NUNES/SHUTTERSTOCK; BIOSPHÈRE DE MONTRÉAL | ESPACE POUR LA VIE

dance floors, playing yard games, kicking back in hammocks and filling up at food trucks serving burgers and poutine. The party takes place by the Jean-Drapeau Métro overlooking the St Lawrence River. Dancing begins around 5pm; crowds twirl until dark. Save money and ensure your entry by purchasing tickets online at least 24 hours in advance.

Splash Through Summer

Between late June and early September, beat summer's heat at **Plage Jean-Doré** *(adult/child/family $8.50/4.50/20.50)*, an artificial gold-sand beach overlooking the lake on Île Notre-Dame. The facilities are safe, clean and ideal for kids, who can splash all day in the 15,000-sq-meter swim zone or hop around **Aquazilla** *(aquazilla.com; per 1hr adult/child/family $22/17/70)*, a

TAKE A BREAK
There's the **Ste-Hélène Bistro-Terrasse** *(11am-6pm Mon-Fri, to 7pm Sat & Sun; $$)* near the Métro and snacks around **Plage Jean-Doré** in summer – largely mediocre. Pack a picnic instead.

SUMMER TRAVEL
Hop on the seasonal ferry from the Old Port to Île Ste-Hélène *(navettesfluviales. com; adult/child $6/free.)* Cyclists can arrive via Pont Jacques-Cartier or the Cité du Havre route.

floating obstacle course. Rent canoes, kayaks, pedal boats or paddle boards *(from $17.25)* to row beyond the beach and explore lagoons within **Jardins des Floralies**, overgrown with greenery.

Scream on a Rollercoaster

Adrenaline junkies go berserk for **La Ronde** *(sixflags.com/larondeen; from $43)*, Québec's largest amusement park, thanks to more than 40 rides and attractions that zoom, spin and drop from mid-May to late October. Though originally built for Expo 67, it's now a Six Flags property, feeling less like a 20th-century historical relic and more like a standard amusement park, fried-food stands and all. Even so, views from atop the coasters can be spectacular – and nothing beats the evening fireworks display, **L'International des Feux Loto-Québec**, which explodes on

Thursdays at 10pm from late June through July. With limited time, don't miss **Le Monstre** – the world's highest dual-tracked wooden coaster, making Montréalers see stars since the 1980s.

Chill Outdoors in Winter

Between late December and March, outdoor enthusiasts can sled down the natural slope near the Métro, cross-country ski through 7km of tree-lined rails or journey through the park on snowshoes and fat bikes. Ice skating is most popular, thanks to a 500m refrigerated trail connected to a large rink where pros let loose. Visit on Saturday evenings for **Slide and Groove** events, when DJs turn the scene into a frosty disco with colorful lights bouncing off the ice. **Patin Patin** *(patinpatin.ca; rentals from $9)* rents equipment for all activities from a shed close to the Métro stop.

Pedal Scenic Pathways

Bike-friendly paths wind through Parc Jean-Drapeau, linking its two islands to mainland Montréal and the St Lawrence's southern shore. Hopping on a BIXI bike can be a fun, fast way to speed through the scenery – just grab wheels near the Jean-Drapeau Métro. Cyclists with a competitive streak should zip to **Circuit Gilles-Villeneuve** – the race track for the Formula 1 Grand Prix du Canada – which opens to cyclists throughout summer.

For a longer journey, try the **14km Bike Link** gliding from Parc Jean-Drapeau along the St Lawrence on a breezy, car-free seaway leading to Ste-Catherine Lock. BIXI won't cut it for this serene riverside ride; rent wheels from **Ça Roule Montreal** *(caroulemontreal.com; from $80)* in the Old Port.

EXPO 67'S LEGACY

Expo 67 – the 1967 International and Universal Exposition celebrating the Canadian Confederation's centennial anniversary – was a major event, with over 50 million people touring nearly 100 pavilions representing 62 nations spread across two river islands over six months. Memories of the Expo live on in the park's public art and repurposed pavilions, like the striking Casino de Montréal.

Explore
Downtown & Chinatown

Researched by John Garry

Downtown (Centre-Ville) slopes from Old Montréal to leafy Mont Royal with office-crammed skyscrapers, wide boulevards and department stores. Most people come to this neighborhood for shows and festivals around Place des Arts or to see some of the city's spectacular museums. The Quartier des Spectacles sits east, where vestiges of Montréal's 20th-century Sin City days linger between cultural centers abutting Chinatown. The Golden Square Mile, Canada's most exclusive 19th-century neighborhood, rises northwest – now the territory of McGill University students, who skip between its remaining mansions on Mont Royal's southern slopes. Rue St-Catherine cuts east-west through it all, a bustling commercial artery.

Getting Around

 Métro
The green line runs east–west through central Downtown with stops at St-Laurent (near MEM), Place-des-Arts, McGill (near Musée McCord Stewart) and Guy-Concordia (near MBAM). The orange line follows the southern edge, with Place-d'Armes providing access to Chinatown.

 Bus
Bus 150 runs east–west along Blvd René-Lévesque. Bus 1 runs along Blvd de Maisonneuve, stopping at Place-des-Arts. Bus 24 goes east–west along Rue Sherbrooke.

 Walk
Beat winter snow and summer rain by walking through the Underground City (p68), a network of Métro-connected tunnels.

THE BEST

LIVE PERFORMANCES
Place des Arts (p64)

WORLD-CLASS ART
Musée des beaux-arts de Montréal (p56)

SOCIAL HISTORIES
MEM (p66)

ASIAN CUISINE
Chinatown (p62)

GILDED MANSIONS
Golden Square Mile (p58)

Chinatown gate (p63)
JTTUCKER/SHUTTERSTOCK

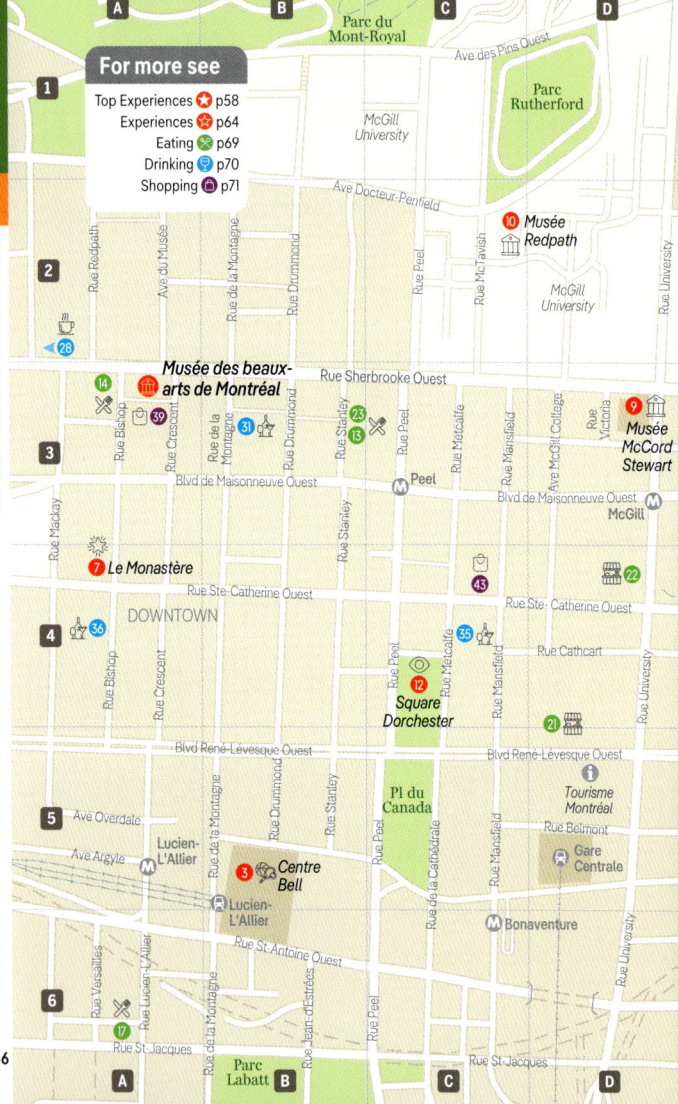

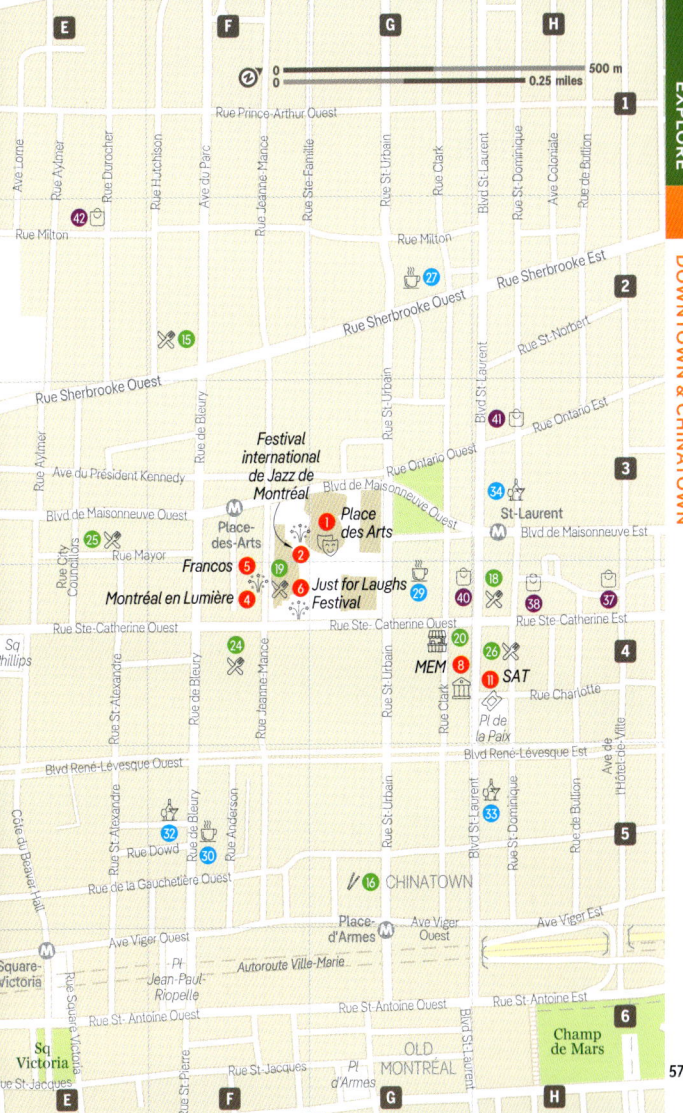

★ TOP EXPERIENCE
Musée des beaux-arts de Montréal

Founded in 1860, The **Musée des beaux-arts de Montréal** (MBAM), also called the Montreal Museum of Fine Arts (MMFA), is an encyclopedic bastion of global creativity with roughly 47,000 works spread around five interconnected pavilions covering 53,000 sq meters. Budget for a few hours.

MAP P58 **A3**

PLANNING TIP
Save $3 by prepurchasing tickets online. Visitors over 26 pay $15 from 5pm to 9pm Wednesdays. Families enter for free from 10am to 1pm Saturday.

Scan the QR code for opening hours and to purchase tickets.

International Connections
Appreciate the museum's immense scope on Level 4 of the **Jean-Noël Desmarais Pavilion**, home of permanent exhibit **The Arts of One World**. Its 10 galleries showcase over 1200 objects covering every continent, spanning the 4th millennium BCE to today. Ancient African masks stare at works by contemporary African artists; Ming Dynasty porcelain appears next to Chinese decor owned by Canada's 19th-century elite. It's a mindful meditation on cultural connectivity across space and time.

Follow this with a crash course in art history around the four-floor **Michael & Renata Hornstein Pavilion for Peace**, with around 500 artworks covering everything from the Middle Ages (Level 4) to the present day (Level 1). Start with Level 1's Impressionists (Matisse, Monet, Renoir) and works by Picasso.

Québécois, Canadian & Indigenous Art
The **Claire & Marc Bourgie Pavilion** celebrates local heritage over six levels spanning the 18th century to the 1980s. Start on Level 4, showcasing Indigenous ingenuity, then make your way down to see Canadian art transform over 400 years.

RECO ALLEYNE/SHUTTERSTOCK

See the work of Canadian modernists on Level 1, including a section dedicated to Marc-Aurèle Fortin, whose whimsical paintings of Québec recall works by Van Gogh. On Level S1, pull out headphones to contemplate Montréal-born Jean-Paul Riopelle's kaleidoscopic abstract mosaics from the 1950s. QR codes connected to three enormous canvases link to electronic instrumentals, designed by Mathieu David Gagnon in 2023 and inspired by Riopelle's work.

Inside the **Michael & Renata Hornstein Pavilion**, peruse art and photographs at ᐅᒻᒪᖅᑐᖅ **uummaqutik: essence of life** – a celebration of Indigenous creativity. Scan the QR code at the entrance to follow the digital audio guide, designed for people with visual impairments and offered in three languages – Inuktitut, French and English.

QUICK BREAK
Hungry? Try **Aube Café** *($)* on Level 2 of the **Jean-Noël Desmarais Pavilion,** or hold out for an Italian sandwich at nearby lunch counter **Mono** *(hours vary; $).*

Stroll the Golden Square Mile

Between 1870 and 1900, palatial homes were built by Canada's wealthy elite along what's now dubbed the Golden Square Mile. Though many mansions were lost to 20th-century development, those that remain hint at the era's extravagance, their grand facades climbing up the slopes of Mont Royal.

START	END	LENGTH
Holt Renfrew Ogilvy	Roddick Gates	2.5km; 1½ hrs

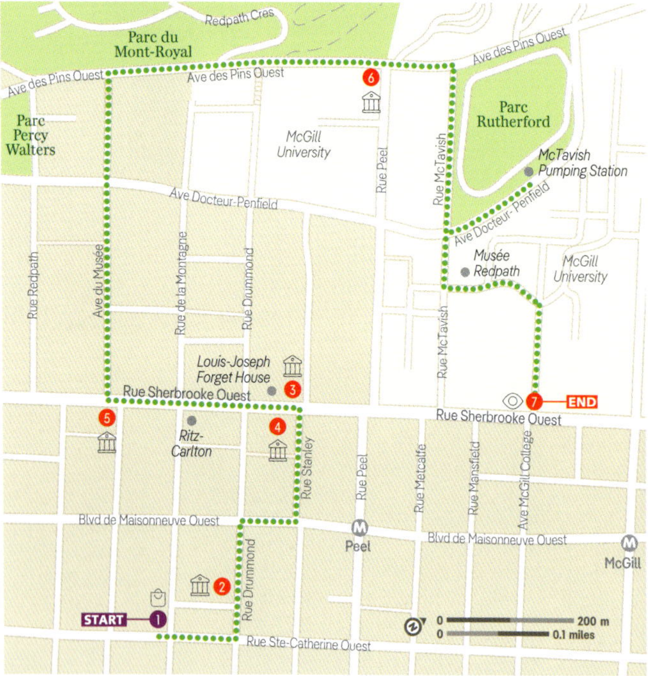

1 Heritage Fashion

Begin at **Holt Renfrew Ogilvy** (holtrenfrew.com), a luxe department store formed by the merger of two heavyweight Canadian retailers: Ogilvy (founded in 1866) and Holt Renfrew (1837). Today, labels like Gucci, Chanel and Dior grace the six-floor complex.

2 Reimagined Mansion

A few blocks away sits **Mount Stephen** (1884), an opulent Italian Renaissance mansion built for Scottish-born tycoon Sir George Stephen, who helped finance the Canadian Pacific Railway. It's now home to a hotel with an elegant restaurant and **Bar George** (bargeorge.ca).

3 Prestigious Club

On Rue Sherbrooke, between Stanley and Drummond, is the **Mount Royal Club**, which splintered from Montréal's St James Club in 1899. The St James was supposedly not exclusive enough. Next door sits the French Second Empire–style Maison Louis-Joseph Forget (1884). Forget, a prominent stockbroker and politician, was one of the first French Canadians to join Montréal's Scottish-dominated aristocracy.

4 Fine Art and Food

The **Maison Alcan** complex rises on Rue Sherbrooke's south side. Push through the art-deco entrance to take in the public atrium, anchored by Mediterranean-inspired **Améa Cafe** (8am-4pm Mon-Fri, from 9am Sat, 10am-3pm Sun; $$).

5 Handsome Hotel

Continue east past the Ritz-Carlton (1912), dubbed the 'Grande Dame of Sherbrooke St,' and head north up Ave du Musée along **MBAM**. The museum's original building – a beaux-arts temple with a white-marble facade (1912) – features symmetrical ionic columns cut and shaped by six men over three months using pneumatic hammers.

6 Elite University

After climbing Ave du Musée's steep steps to Ave des Pins, walk east to McGill University past the turreted, Queen Anne Revival–style **Maison Lady Meredith** (1897), part of the McGill campus. In 1813, Scottish fur trader James McGill bequeathed a 46-acre estate to start the school, which opened in 1829 and is now one of Canada's most prestigious universities.

7 Graystone and Skyscrapers

Wind downhill into campus life, passing the château-esque McTavish pumping station (1932), which dominates Parc Rutherford's southern edge, and the Greek Revival Musée Redpath (1882), built from local graystone. End at **Roddick Gates** (1924), a grand archway separating yesteryear's glamor from Downtown's modern skyscrapers.

WALKING TOUR

Sample Chinatown's Cuisine

In 1902, French-language newspaper *La Presse* first used the term 'Quartier Chinois' to reference Chinatown. The neighborhood has morphed since then, now a tiny tourist-friendly area framed by red-and-gold paifang gates. Despite its size, the options for Asian cuisine seem endless. Come hungry.

START	END	LENGTH
Blvd St-Laurent and Blvd René-Lévesque	Restaurant Chinatown Kim Fung	500m; 2 hrs

1 Colorful Entrance
Enter the micro-neighborhood through its **northern gate** on Blvd St-Laurent and gaze at the mural facing Blvd René-Lévesque. Entitled *May an Old Song Open a New World* (2015), and featuring a Chinese opera singer holding a lily, it's the work of artists Bryan Beyung and Gene Pendon.

2 Tastes of Vietnam
Bite into Vietnamese tradition at **Hoang Oanh** *(10am-6pm; $)*. Fill up on its signature banh mi (a baguette sandwich stuffed with your choice of meat or tofu and smothered in mayonnaise) or grab a handheld banh bao (an eggy, garlic-seasoned pork bun) to eat on the street.

3 Delicious Dumplings
Find a table at **Qing Hua Dumplings** *(11am-9:30pm Sun-Thu, to 10pm Fri & Sat; $)* serving over 30 types of its namesake flavor bombs. Each order comes with 15 dumplings – get a pack to share, dunking them in vinegar, soy sauce or hot chili oil.

4 Sweet Treats
For Chinese baked goods with Parisian panache, hop across the street to **Pâtisserie Coco** *(9am-8pm Sun-Thu, to 9pm Fri & Sat; $)* and pick up a tray to collect your treats – perhaps custard buns, black-sesame brioche loaves or packets of chewy mochi.

5 Ancient Candies
There are more sweets at **Dragon Beard Candy** *(12:30-4:30pm Mon-Thu, to 7pm Sat & Sun; $)*, a bite-size counter making teeny confections dating back to China's Han Dynasty. Watch as the Candy Master repeatedly pulls sugar dough, creating thousands of strands – a 'dragon's beard' – used to wrap a peanut-sesame-chocolate-coconut filling.

6 Pillowy Pockets
To taste some more tempting desserts, pop into **Pâtisserie Bao Bao Dim Sum** *(10am-6pm; $)*, serving warm, chewy treats packed with flavors like lotus root and red-bean paste, along with savory meat-packed buns.

7 Noodles Galore
Still hungry? Stop at the **Noodle Factory** *(noon-9pm Wed-Sun; $)*, a cash-only spot where chef Lin Kwong Cheung whacks and kneads hand-pulled noodles into delicate strips. If you like heat, don't skimp on the sweet house-made hot sauce.

8 Dim Sum Dining
Hidden up an escalator in the rear of shopping mall Place du Quartier is **Restaurant Chinatown Kim Fung** *(8am-3pm & 5-10pm; $$)*. Come here for Cantonese dim sum and Sichuan platters, which servers roll out on trolleys to entice diners.

EXPERIENCES

Applaud at Place des Arts
PERFORMING ARTS

MAP: ① P57 G3

Place des Arts (*placedesarts.com*), Canada's largest performing arts complex, spreads across six different halls at the heart of Quartier des Spectacles. With roughly 900 shows and events attended by a million spectators annually, there's a little something for everyone.

For the classically inclined, try **Opéra de Montréal** (*operademontreal.com*), North America's biggest francophone opera house, presenting everything from traditional scores to contemporary pieces sung by a mix of Canadian and international vocalists. Performances take place in the acoustically astounding Salle Wilfrid-Pelletier hall. There are 30% discounts on tickets for those aged 18-34.

This hall is also where point-perfect ballerinas twirl for the **Grands Ballets Canadiens** (*grandsballets.com*), Québec's first professional ballet company. Of the company's six annual shows, *The Nutcracker* is a perennial favorite, delighting holiday audiences with Montréal-born choreographer Fernand Nault's take on Tchaikovsky's score since 1964. The 18-34 crowd receives 40% discounts. Symphony orchestras, contemporary dance, comedy and theater performances round out the offerings.

Jam to Live Jazz
FESTIVALS AND CONCERTS

MAP: ② P57 F3

In the 1920s, jazz music jumped the US border and migrated to Montréal. Its rebellious rhythms poured from clubs like champagne, seeping into Montréal's sonic landscape. Though its popularity waned in the 1960s and '70s, the 1980 launch of **Festival international de Jazz de Montréal** (*montrealjazzfest.com*) sparked a revival. It's now the world's largest jazz fest, with around 3000 musicians giving 500 performances across 10 days between late June and early July. Some 350 of those concerts are alfresco jam sessions outside Place des Arts – all free for the public.

For quality jazz outside of June's jamboree, try **Upstairs Jazz Bar & Grill** (*upstairsjazz.com*), which hosts everyone in its cozy club from local legend Jim Doxas to McGill University's finest students. Check the schedule and reserve seats online to ensure admittance. There are usually one to three sets per night; lesser-known acts are often gratis. Come hungry – there's a full dinner menu (burgers, steak, nachos).

Go Coocoo for Canadiens at the Centre Bell
LIVE SPORTS

MAP: ③ P56 B5

Montréal's love of hockey runs deeper than Québec's maple syrup reserves, so it's no surprise the highest-capacity arena in the National Hockey League (NHL) sits smack-dab in the city's center. The **Centre Bell** *(centrebell.ca)* seats over 21,000 hockey heads, who gather in Hab gear from October to April to cheer on the Canadiens. ('Hab,' the Canadiens' nickname, is short for 'Habitants' in French, which translates to 'settlers' – referencing the province's early French inhabitants). If you want to see the home team play live, score tickets online *(nhl.com/canadiens)* and show up early – doors open 90 minutes before scheduled matches, and you can grab drinks and food within the arena.

If a game isn't on the cards, opt for an hour-long Centre Bell walking tour *(centrebell.ca/en/guided-tours; adult/child $22/13)* to get a close-up of the arena where Canadiens fight for puck supremacy and backstage spaces.

See Circus at Le Monastère
ACROBATS AND CLOWNS

MAP: P56 **A4**

Catch death-defying acts at **Le Monastère** *(le-monastere.ca; from $37.50)*, which transforms a 19th-century neo-Gothic church into a non-religious circus cabaret. It's set up like theater-in-the-round, with performers on a central stage ascending heavens-high on everything from silks to trapeze and stacked chairs. The cabaret's comedic relief usually performs in French, but don't worry: there's no language barrier when it comes to physical comedy.

Arrive 20 to 30 minutes before curtain to enjoy the full experience. Grab a bag of popcorn, order an adult beverage and get ready to watch talented acrobats soar among the rafters.

FANTASTIC DOWNTOWN FESTIVALS

Montréal en Lumière
MAP: 4 P57 **F4**

Brightens Montréal's darkest months with food, live performances, illuminated art and an outdoor skating rink. It coincides with Nuit Blanche *(nuitblanchemtl.com)*, a one-night arts festival that doesn't quit till dawn. *(Feb-Mar; montrealenlumiere.com)*

Francos
MAP: 5 P57 **F4**

Hosts around 150 French-language music concerts over nine days as summer heats the city. *(Jun; francosmontreal.com)*

Just for Laughs
MAP: 6 P57 **F4**

Brings stand-ups to town for the world's biggest comedy fest. *(Jul; montreal.hahaha.com)*

Meet All Kinds of Montréalers at MEM
SOCIAL STORIES MUSEUM

MAP: ⑧ P57 G4

What makes Montréal tick? Centre des mémoires montréalaises, or **MEM** *(memmtl.ca; adult/child $15.50/free)*, provides answers through interactive exhibits and mini documentaries that span centuries of history. No fluff here – permanent exhibit *Montréal* digs deep, featuring around 100 firsthand accounts from a diversity of locals. You might hear from a *dépanneur* owner, spin around town with a disability activist or learn a few Franglish phrases. Rotating exhibits use an equally thoughtful, human-first approach to storytelling. It's closed Mondays.

If you're short on time or pinching pennies, the free-to-visit 2nd-floor lobby is still worth exploring. It's packed with hands-on maps, fast facts and a 13-minute movie about the evolution of Blvd St-Laurent, where MEM is located. Best of all, this museum is accessible for people with limited mobility, ensuring this museum about everyone welcomes everyone, too.

Explore the Musée McCord Stewart
HISTORY AND CULTURE

MAP: ⑨ P56 D3

Sift through centuries of Canada's social history at this **midsize museum** *(musee-mccord-stewart.ca; adult/child $20/free)* near McGill University. The collection consists of over 1.5 million artifacts – one of North America's largest historical collections – with fashion, photography, paintings, decorative arts and more all on display. Budget for an hour or two; buy tickets online to save money. It's closed Mondays.

Indigenous Voices Today, the permanent 1st-floor exhibit, ruminates on centuries of Indigenous life in Canada, with artifacts and testimonies from First Nations people reflecting on cultural knowledge and colonial trauma. Rotating exhibits, located on the top two floors, examine local history, with past exhibits covering topics such as Montréal's

---

WHEN MONTRÉAL BURNED RED

In the 1920s, Montréal was a town of vice where you could find burlesque, betting houses – and, most importantly, booze. The city never enacted Prohibition laws, so alcohol flowed freely, drawing tap-happy tipplers from the neighboring US. Mobsters ruled the roost, prostitution ran rampant and the area around Rue Ste-Catherine, running through today's Quartier des Spectacles and the Quartier Latin, was dubbed the Red Light District. By the 1950s, officials started scrubbing Montréal's streets, and by the early 2000s there was little left of this promiscuous past – save for Café Cleopatra, a storied strip joint where the red lights still flicker.

19th-century costume balls and the transformation of Little Burgundy's Black community.

On-site **Cafe Notman** – named after 19th-century Canadian photographer William Notman, whose work decorates the walls – sells filling lunch fare. When weather permits, take your food to eat outside at **Museum Alley,** a yellow-pink-blue take on Montréal's *ruelles vertes* (green alleys, p31).

Nerd Out at Musée Redpath   NATURAL HISTORY
MAP: 10 P56 C2

There's a touch of Hogwartsian magic to the natural history collection at McGill University's **Musée Redpath** *(mcgill.ca/redpath; by donation)*. It's less stodgy museum and more cabinet of curiosities, with hodgepodge exhibits related to paleontology, zoology and mineralogy scattered across three floors. Find the 2.5-million-year-old *Australopithecus africanus* skull near an ancient Egyptian mummy, seemingly uncoiling behind its glass case (Floor 3). Then, hunt for taxidermied animals with Canadian pedigree before stumbling upon an ancient woolly mammoth hair and a table piled with glittering rocks (Floor 2). The museum is closed Sundays and Mondays.

Views from the 3rd-floor wraparound balcony are particularly striking, staring down the toothy grin of a gorgosaurus from the Late Cretaceous Epoch. The Greek Revival graystone structure, completed in 1882, is equally mesmerizing – and one of the nation's oldest museum buildings. Search the museum's west-side base stones and you might spot 470-million-year-old fossils hidden in the facade – fitting for a house of natural science.

Dance Under SAT's Dome   CONCERTS AND COFFEE
MAP: P57 H4

It's all about the visuals at nonprofit **Société des Arts Technologiques** *(sat.qc.ca)*, called SAT, a 44,000-sq-ft creative incubator where art, technology and music collide. Most people come here to get lost in the Satosphere, a convex concert hall with an 18m-diameter dome and 157 loudspeakers delivering immersive, 360-degree audiovisual experiences. It's soundtracked by DJs spinning genre-spanning sets, with a heavy focus on EDM (check the schedule to see what's on and purchase tickets).

Not up for a full-on dance party? Get a jolt of energy at the connected **Café SAT** *(8am-5pm Mon-Thu, to 10pm Fri)*, serving its fruit-forward house brew (made in collaboration with Montréal roaster Jungle) alongside a small food menu. Show up on Fridays from 5pm to 10pm, when the cafe turns into an electronic listening room with DJs spinning tunes for crowds sipping microbrews.

UNDERGROUND CITY

You'd never know it while strutting Downtown's sidewalks, but hidden underground is a 33km network of subterranean tunnels linking the Métro to 2000-plus shops, restaurants, apartment buildings, hotels, offices, museums and entertainment complexes. This is Underground City, officially called **RÉSO (Réseau de la Ville Souterraine)**. It first appears like a run-of-the-mill shopping mall – a disappointment if you're imagining a magical metropolis – but it's a remarkable feat of civil engineering, dating back to 1964 and dotted with public art, including a piece of the Berlin Wall. Roughly 500,000 Montréalers pass through it daily – a welcome reprieve from the city's weather extremes.

Spin Around Square Dorchester ARCHITECTURE AND GHOSTS

MAP: 12 P56 C4

For an architectural eyeful, stand atop one of the Venetian-inspired bridges on the northern corner of leafy **Square Dorchester**. To the north is the **Dominion Square Building** (1930) – a Lombard Romanesque Revival heavyweight with a limestone facade. To the east, the hulking beaux-arts **Sun Life Building** (1914–33) rises 122m into the sky – the largest edifice in the British Empire upon completion. Look for the 13 statues perched on top of **Cathédrale Marie-Reine-du-Monde** (1870–94; *mariereinedumonde.org*) – diagonally across from the park's southeastern corner – one of the city's four basilicas. Modeled after St Peter's basilica in Rome, the baroque beauty forms the shape of a cross, covering 4700 sq meters.

Placards on building facades offer more detailed architectural and historical information, along with a numbered map highlighting more intriguing structures nearby. Then there's the history you can't see. Thousands of bodies supposedly rest under the park, remnants of Square Dorchester's days as a 19th-century cemetery for cholera victims. Latin crosses in the pavement mark the graveyard's presence.

LISTINGS

Best Places for...

❶ Budget ❷❷ Midrange ❸❸❸ Top End

Eating

Cafes with Breakfast & Lunch

Caffettiera ❶
⓭ B3
Get a proper Italian espresso in this peppy color-blocked cafe and *aperitivo* bar with Italian pastries and focaccia sandwiches. *caffettiera.ca, 7:30am-6pm*

Cafe Aunja ❶
⓮ A3
'There' (*aunja* in Farsi) delivers a taste of Iran with rose-flavored teas, tisanes and sandwiches a few blocks from MBAM. *aunja.com, 9am-7:30pm Mon-Fri, 10am-7pm Sat, to 6pm Sun*

Mintar ❶
⓯ F2
Head upstairs to watch staff prep smoothie bowls, salads, coffees and flat top–grilled sammies in the open kitchen below. *mintar.ca, hours vary*

Splurge-worthy Dinners

Fleurs et Cadeaux ❸❸❸
⓰ G5
Sake pours from tinted bottles and diners sit at a rectangular bar as staff meticulously prepare bite-sized Japanese dishes. Speakeasy Sans Soleil hides downstairs. *fleursetcadeaux.com, 5-10:30pm*

Nora Gray ❸❸❸
⓱ A6
Fork into velvety pasta ribbons and shareable plates in this Italian-inspired joint with bitters-forward cocktails and exceptional service. *noragray.com, 5-10pm Tue-Thu, to 10:30pm Fri & Sat*

Cadet ❸❸❸
⓲ H4
Down-at-heel St-Laurent gets sophisticated at this industrial, softly lit preshow destination with tapas-style veggie plates and fish, along with a fantastic wine menu. *restaurantcadet.com, 5-11pm*

Kamùy ❷❷
⓳ F4
Sail from Place des Arts to the West Indies in this glass-walled restaurant with a terrace for reinvented Caribbean classics such as jerk chicken. *kamuy.ca, 5-10:30pm Wed-Sun*

Food Markets

Le Central ❷❷
⓴ G4
Search for international cuisine inside this industrial Quartier des Spectacles center with long communal tables. *lecentral.ca, hours vary*

Le Cathcart ❷❷
㉑ D4
An enormous skylight lets sun into this upmarket Underground City food court, packed with Downtown's white-collar crowd at lunchtime. *lecathcart.com, hours vary*

Time Out Market ❷❷
㉒ D4
Counters representing popular Montréal restaurants serve Thai, Japanese, Indian and more on the Centre

Eaton's 2nd floor. *timeout.com, hours vary*

Vegan & Vegetarian-friendly

Le Taj 🅢🅢
23 B3

Expect Indian authenticity in each bite, perfected since 1985. The clay wall panels were created for Expo 67. *restaurantletaj.com, 5-10:30pm Sun-Thu, to 11pm Fri & Sat*

Bloom Sushi 🅢🅢
24 F4

Each piece of plant-based sushi is a flavor explosion, as delicate and exciting as cherry blossoms bursting in springtime. *bloomsushi.com, hours vary*

Unfussy Dining

Cafe Parvis 🅢🅢
25 E3

Kick back in this two-floor parlor with 1970s pizzazz for pizza, sandwiches, coffee and wine – hidden a block from bustling Rue Ste-Catherine. *cafeparvis.com, hours vary*

Montréal Pool Room 🅢
26 H4

Billiards? *Non.* Steamed hot dogs (called *steamés*)? *Oui.* Order yours all-dressed, with onion, cabbage and mustard. *montrealpoolroom1912.com. 10:30am-4am*

Drinking

Stylish Cafes

Osmo x Murasan
27 G2

Enjoy java and Japanese-influenced drinks beneath the disco ball in this space-age bunker spinning electro tunes, or on the outdoor patio in warm weather. *marusan.ca, 8am-6pm Mon-Fri, 10am-6pm Sat & Sun*

Côte Café
28 A2

Teeny-weeny Côte grinds beans from local roaster Zab, best enjoyed on its streetside patio a few blocks west of MBAM. *@cotemtl, 6am-6pm*

Café Tranquille
29 G4

Overlook the crowds on Esplanade Tranquille from this second-story cafe with generous seating and two terraces – ideal for warming up after skating on the outdoor ice rink in winter. *quartierdesspectacles.com, 10am-10:30pm*

La Finca
30 F5

UQAM's kids love this airy cafe with brunch fare and a tiny market of artisanal wine, beer, coffee beans and quirky cards, located on the Old Montréal-Downtown border. *lafinca.ca, 8am-4pm*

Craft Cocktails

Cloakroom
31 B3

A men's tailoring store guards this slender, no-menu speakeasy where bartenders craft made-to-measure cocktails. How fitting. Expect a wait on weekends. *cloakroombarmtl.com, 4pm-1am Sun-Thu, to 3am Fri & Sat*

Sans Soleil
see **16** G5

Tables by the DJ booth vanish around 10pm as dancers take over this Japanese-influenced spot beneath Fleurs et Cadeaux. *sanssoleilmtl.com, 6:30pm-1am Mon-Wed, to 2:30am Thu-Sun*

Club Pelicano
32 F5

Splash into craft cocktails inside this art-deco, pool-themed, below-ground bar where DJs spin tunes; upstairs is Peruvian seafood restaurant Tiradito. *clubpelicano.com, hours vary*

Laidback Bars

Poincaré
33 H5

Beers are artisanal, fries are fermented and the seasonal rooftop pulses at night atop this 2nd-floor Chinatown lair. *poincare chinatown.com, 4pm-1am Sun-Wed, to 2am Thu-Sat*

Bar Pamplemousse
 H3

Order 5oz pours to sample some of the 20-odd beers on tap at this tavern with Mediterranean bites. *barpamplemousse.com, 4:30pm-1am Sun-Thu, to 2am Fri & Sat*

Bar Dominion
35 C4

If this storied wood-and-tile tavern's taps could talk, they'd sing of the original 1927 hotel restaurant and a century of revelry. In addition to cocktails, there's a fantastic pub-style menu specializing in seafood. *dominionmtl.com, 4pm-1am*

Grumpys Bar
 A4

Reading works by Montréal's Mordecai Richler? Toast the late author at the dimly lit dive he supposedly loved. *@grumpysbar, 5pm-1am Sun & Mon, 3pm-3am Tue-Sat*

Shopping

Time-tested Stores

Henri Henri
37 H4

A leather-scented hat supplier selling all styles of *chapeaux* since 1932. Master hat-maker Sylvain Labbé, a former Cirque du Soleil designer, crafts bespoke fits for all sizes. *henrihenri.ca, 10am-6pm Mon-Fri, to 5pm Sat & Sun*

Pantalons Supérieurs
 H4

Established in 1924, 'Superior Pants' is a family-owned jean shop where denim dynamo Mitch Stroll helps customers find the perfect fit. Offers on-site alterations. *9:30am-6pm Mon-Fri, to 5pm Sat*

Divine Chocolatier
39 A3

Sugar fiends started flocking to this shop owned by Belgian chocolatier Richard Zwierzynski in 1976. Warm up with a cup of creamy hot chocolate in winter. *divinechocolatier. com, 11am-6pm Tue-Fri, to 5pm Sat & Sun*

Indiana Jeans
40 G4

In 1991 this boutique transformed a corner of Blvd St-Laurent into the Wild West with boots, jeans, buckles and bags. *@indianajeansmtl, noon-6pm Mon-Wed & Sat, to 7pm Thu & Fri, to 5pm Sun*

Upcycled Fashion & Books

Eva B
41 H3

This vintage store started stuffing its shop with all sorts of treasures in the 1980s, like Hawaiian shirts, Cabbage Patch dolls, rollerblades and prom dresses primed for a second chance to dance. *boutiqueevab.com, 11am-7pm Mon-Sat, to 6pm Sun*

The Word
42 E2

A living-room-sized bookstore open since 1975, where you may find Balzac collectibles, Harry Potter in Latin and plenty of French and English titles. *thewordbookstore.ca, 10am-8pm Mon-Wed, to 9pm Thu & Fri, to 6pm Sat*

International Labels

La Maison Simons
43 C4

Originally a Québec City dry goods shop founded in 1840, this fashion retailer now sells stylish duds at department stores nationwide, including a spacious Ste-Catherine outlet. *simons.ca, hours vary*

See p84 for eating, drinking and shopping listings

Explore
Quartier Latin, the Village & HoMa

Researched by
John Garry

Rue St-Denis is the place to be in the Quartier Latin, its sidewalks sprinkled with an array of Université du Québec à Montréal (UQAM) students and theatergoers, plus people confronting the realities of homelessness and addiction. The Village (also called the Gay Village) comes alive once night descends, with dance clubs and LGBTIQ+ bars along Rue Ste-Catherine bumping from dinner till dawn. Further east, there's up-and-coming Hochelaga-Maisonneuve (HoMa). Though the 1976 Olympics put this industrial francophone neighborhood on the map, its renaissance has only recently arrived. Explore the residential area's artisanal revitalization before seeing the natural science museums around Parc Olympique, each an architectural eyeful.

Getting Around

 Métro

Orange, green and yellow lines stop at Berri-UQAM in the Quartier Latin; green continues east to Beaudry and Papineau in the Village, then on to Pie-IX and Viau for Parc Olympique and HoMa.

 Bus

In the Village, bus 24 runs east–west along Sherbrooke (to the north); bus 34 runs east–west along Ste-Catherine (to the south). In the Quartier Latin, bus 30 runs north–south along Rues Berri and St-Denis.

 Walk

Rue Ste-Catherine links Downtown, the Quartier Latin and the Village.

Rue Ste-Catherine (p85)
MARC BRUXELLE/ALAMY

THE BEST

NATURAL WONDERS
Biodôme (p77)

WORKING-CLASS HISTORY
Ecomusée du fier monde (p82)

ELEGANT ARCHITECTURE
Château Dufresne (p83)

ARTISANAL EATS
Aube Boulangerie (p83)

LGBTIQ+ NIGHTLIFE
Rue Ste-Catherine (p85)

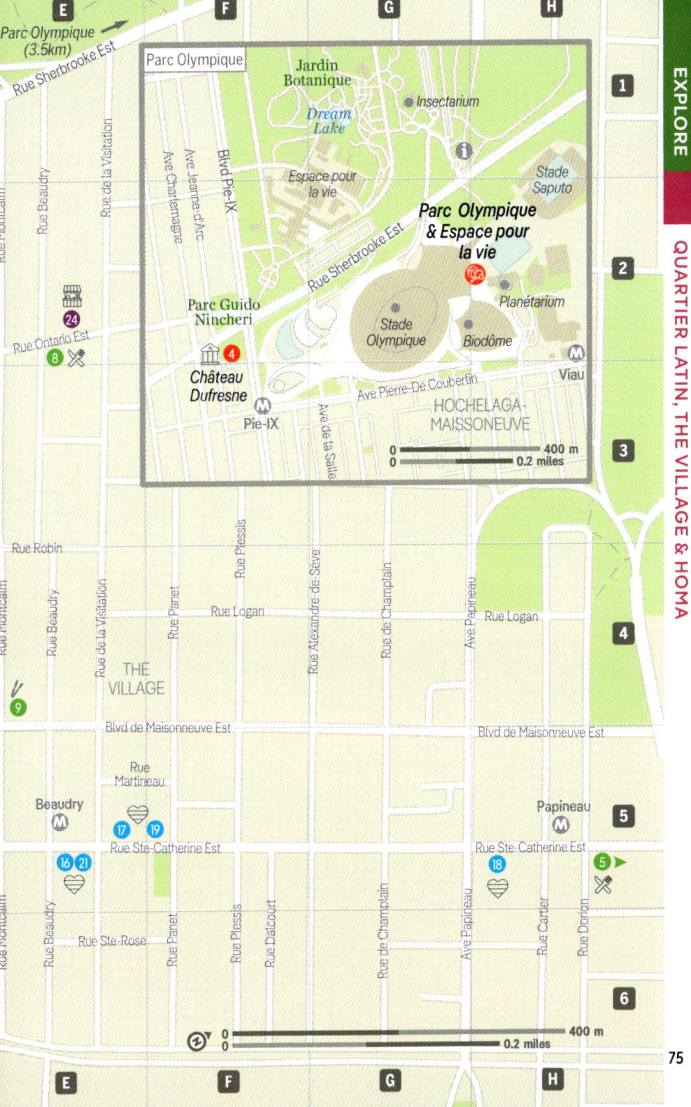

★ **TOP EXPERIENCE**

Parc Olympique & Espace pour la vie

Four museums, a leaning tower from the 1976 Olympics and green spaces linking them all: no one's getting bored at **Parc Olympique**, central to **Espace pour la vie** (Space for Life; *espacepourlavie.ca*), Canada's largest natural science complex. See the exhibits or walk the grounds to appreciate the architecture.

MAP P75 **G2**

PLANNING TIP
Seeing one of Espace pour la vie's museums can take at least an hour. Add a second stop and budget half a day. Wear comfortable shoes and bring layers for the journey.

Scan the QR code for museum hours and to purchase tickets.

Stade Olympique

Constructed for the 1976 Summer Olympics, this **stadium** (*parcolympique.qc.ca*) is an impressive monument to Montréal's mid-20th-century architectural ambitions. It has two nicknames: the Big O, for 'Olympics,' and the Big Owe, for taxpayers, who saw the cost of the Games balloon from an initial $120 million to $1.47 billion by the time the city paid it off three decades later.

The stadium is dominated by the 165m-high **Montréal Tower** (pictured), which extends over HoMa at a 45-degree angle, making it the tallest inclined tower in the world. A new glass-cabin funicular is set to open to the public in 2027, whisking riders to an observation deck for a sweeping island panorama.

On the first weekends of June, July and August, come hungry for **Les Premiers Vendredis** (*lespremiersvendredis.ca*), Canada's largest food truck gathering, which packs Parc Olympique's esplanade (outside the stadium) and the **Old Port** (p39) with snack stands dishing up all kinds of cuisine.

AWANA JF/SHUTTERSTOCK

Biodôme

From outside, the **Biodôme** looks like an enormous dinosaur egg – fitting for this 'House of Life', constructed as the velodrome (cycling track) for the '76 Olympics. The space now features five of America's ecosystems under one roof, with 2500 animals representing around 200 species. Wave to capybaras in a **Tropical Rainforest**, see what's lurking underwater around the **Gulf of St Lawrence** and observe otters playing in the **Laurentian Maple Forest**. You can also hop alongside puffins on the **Labrador Coast** and waddle with penguins around the **Sub-Antarctic Islands**. Set aside a couple of hours, visit midweek to avoid crowds

TAKE A BREAK
For eco-friendly snacks, grab vegan bites from **Espace Végo** *(9am-5pm Tue-Sun; $)* inside the Planétarium and Biodôme. A seasonal cafe-terrace at Jardin Botanique offers filling vegetarian plates.

SEE MORE FOR LESS
To see **Espace pour la vie**'s museums, including Parc Jean-Drapeau's **Biosphère**, but not **Stade Olympique**, save money with a SOLO Passport ($87; bigger discounts for families).

and follow the self-guided circuit to ensure you see everything.

Planétarium

The **Planétarium**, shaped like a pair of whirling sci-fi spaceships facing the Biodôme, hurls visitors light-years from Earth inside two domed theaters featuring movies about astronomy. Films skew kid-friendly. (Recent flicks traveled to the icy dunes of Mars and explored distant planets throughout the Milky Way). Ensure you reserve tickets for the correct language: films are offered in English and French on a rotating schedule. Choose one film or a double feature.

An underground hallway connects the Planétarium and the Biodôme.

VINCENT JIANG/SHUTTERSTOCK; JARDIN BOTANIQUE DE MONTRÉAL | ESPACE POUR LA VIE

Insectarium

See the world from a bug's point of view inside this dynamically designed **museum** housing thousands of living and preserved insects. Budding entomologists enjoy burrowing underground to a suite of interactive exhibits, while adults appreciate the 9m domed cathedral lined with 3000 framed specimens – one row arranged chromatically, another grouped by categories like 'Impressive Legs.' Most magnificent is the **Great Vivarium**, a sawtooth-topped greenhouse where butterflies emerge from chrysalises to flutter freely through the air. The scene is spectacular in winter – a warm jungle oasis in the middle of frost-bitten Montréal.

Jardin Botanique

Open since the 1930s, the **Jardin Botanique** *(amisjardin.com)* has blossomed into the world's third-largest botanic garden, with 10 exhibition greenhouses and 20 outdoor gardens covering 75 hectares. Admire Ming dynasty design around the **Chinese Garden**'s Lac de Rêve (Dream Lake; pictured), get in touch with Indigenous foliage around the **First Nations Garden** and glide through the **Japanese Garden** with its traditional pavilions, tea room and the largest bonsai 'forest' outside Asia. Visit between May and October, when seasonal petals turn outdoor exhibits into natural art shows.

GET A GUIDE
Download the Espace pour la vie app for visits to the **Biôdome** and **Insectarium**, which trade interpretive museum signs for digital guides. **Jardin Botanique** offers free outdoor guided tours *(10.30am & 1.30pm daily May-Oct)* and indoor guided tours that visit the Marie-Victorin Herbarium and the Biodiversity Center *(1.30pm Wed year-round)*.

Saunter Through the Gayborhood

Montréal's annual Pride parade – Fierté Montréal (*fiertemontreal.com*), held in early August – is the largest LGBTIQ+ gathering in the francophone world. But the road to queer acceptance wasn't always paved with rainbows. Explore the city's pink past on this short stroll.

START	END	LENGTH
Église St-Pierre-Apôtre	L'Euguélionne	1km; 1 hr

1. Lavender History

Ponder Christianity's influence on queer Montréal outside **Église St-Pierre-Apôtre** *(diocesemontreal.org)*. In 1648 an unnamed military drummer with the French garrison was charged with 'crimes of the worst kind' – a phrase used to describe homosexual acts. Québec's Catholic Bishop offered him two options: become executioner or receive the death penalty. The musician chose the former.

2. Prayers for All

Step inside St-Pierre-Apôtre and pay your respects at the **Chapel of Hope** – inaugurated in 1996 this was the world's first chapel dedicated to victims of AIDS. The illness devastated Montréal's LGBTIQ+ community.

3. Solemn Memorial

Head to **Parc de l'Espoir** (Park of Hope) on the corner of Rues Panet and Ste-Catherine, founded in 1991 by ACT UP Montréal as a memorial for those lost to HIV/AIDS in Québec. For years, mourners tied ribbons inscribed with the names of loved ones to trees here. Today, a red ribbon embedded in the ground keeps their spirit alive.

4. Queer Gear

Veer west on Rue Ste-Catherine, passing street poles decorated in tubular Pride flags, en route to **Priape** *(priape.com)*. When this emporium specializing in hand-crafted leather fetish gear and adult toys opened in 1974, it marked the gayborhood's gradual move from Downtown to the Village.

5. Dine and Drink

Order a cocktail at **Renard**. Hanging out in LGBTIQ+ establishments such as this wasn't always easy. In 1977, police stormed Downtown's now-defunct leather bar Truxx and nearby Le Mystique, arresting 146 men on trumped-up morality charges. The next day, over 2000 protesters flooded the streets. By year's end, Québec became Canada's first province to ban sexual orientation-based discrimination.

6. ROY-G-BIV Art

Continue on Ste-Catherine to the **Beaudry Métro station**, outfitted with rainbow pillars in 1999, and look for *Le Rêve de Ron Farha* (*The Dream of Ron Farha*), a mural by street artist XRAY. Ron's dream? A march through Montréal raising HIV/AIDS awareness. His legacy lives on through the charitable Farha Foundation *(fqsida.org)*.

7. LGBTIQ+ Authors

End inside **L'Euguélionne** *(librairieleuguelionne.com)*, a queer feminist bookstore stocked with French and English literature, including stellar zines. Pick up a pamphlet by a contemporary artist to uncover the city's latest LGBTIQ+ stories.

EXPERIENCES

Meet the Working Class at Ecomusée du fier monde
HISTORY MUSEUM

MAP: ① P74 D2

Montréal's blue-collar crowd gets its due at this **museum** *(ecomusee.qc.ca; adult/child $14/8)* inside an ex-bathhouse. Permanent exhibit **All the Livelong Day! The Joys and Sorrows of Life in a Working-Class Neighbourhood** examines the rise, fall and current reinvention of Centre-Sud, a 20th-century nabe now split into a patchwork of communities, including the Village. Visitors loop around the balcony – which overlooks the bathhouse's former pool – to see photos, artifacts and multimedia displays that show the daily life of laboring families who kept Montréal's industrial era factories afloat. Allow 45 minutes to take it all in; it's closed Mondays and Tuesdays.

Between its brick facade and cathedral-worthy ceiling, the building's 1927 art-deco bones are arguably the museum's greatest assets. In 1905 the City of Montréal estimated 75% of working-class homes lacked places to bathe. Public bathhouses like this one – formerly the Bain Généreux – became important community hubs.

Watch Canadian Films at Cinémathèque Québécoise
CINEMA AND GALLERY

MAP: ② P74 A4

Join cinephiles by sinking into seats to watch avant-garde films, animated shorts and cult classics at this **theater** *(cinematheque.qc.ca; adult/child $13/11)*, founded in 1963 to safeguard Québec's audio-visual heritage. New releases get screened in concert with footage from the institution's impressive archive, which holds 40,000 films and videos, and 30,000 television broadcasts. Most movies showcase Québec makers, with plenty of Canadian directors and international Quartier Latin, the Village & HoMas in the mix.

In addition to screenings, there's a series of free-to-visit art exhibits throughout the year, presenting new works alongside selections from the vault's exhaustive collection of posters and photographs.

Head to the cafe pre- or post-film to discuss your favorite Québec directors over coffee, beer or wine. In May, check out **Sommets du Cinéma d'Animation** *(sommetsanimation.com)*, a five-day animated film festival.

Clap for Classic Drag at Cabaret Mado
LIVE PERFORMANCE

MAP: ③ P74 D5

Hairline-high eyebrows, puckered lips and a wardrobe screaming 'clown chic' – that's what to expect when Montréal drag pioneer Mado Lamotte takes the stage at her eponymous **Rue Ste-Catherine cabaret** *(mado.qc.ca; tickets from $34)*. Mado – who goes by Luc Provost offstage – started treading the boards in 1987, long before *RuPaul's Drag Race Canada* sashayed onto TV screens. Don't expect death drops – she saves those tricks for her roster of younger performers. Lamotte, instead, is a cunning bilinguist, serving as impresario at her intimate venue.

Plan your visit to see the long-running **Mado Reçoit**, with a rotating cast of queens ranging from schlocky to exceptional, and purchase tickets in advance to ensure admittance. Unlike many establishments along Rue Ste-Catherine, this isn't a gay bar; crowds tend to be female-forward. Save your bills: though tipping is normal at most drag shows, you're not expected to toss loonies and toonies at this talent.

Eat Artisanal in HoMa FOOD TOUR
MAP: ⑤ P75 **H5**

Hochelaga-Maisonneuve, the working-class area south of Parc Olympique, is having a renaissance. Begin this mini food and drink tour at **Aube Boulangerie** (*aubeboulangerie.com; 7am-6pm; $*), where you can watch bakers prep croissants, financiers, scones and baby-sized bread loaves.

Take sweets to go and head to **Marché Maisonneuve** (*marches publics-mtl.com; 9am-6pm Tue-Sat, to 5pm Sun & Mon; $*) where bakers, butchers, fishmongers and cheese connoisseurs sell snacks. After finding something tasty, grab a table inside or a bench at neighboring Parc Morgan to enjoy your feast. With your picnic polished off, stop by local bean-to-bar chocolatier **Qantu** (*qantuchocolate.com, 10am-5pm Mon-Fri, 11am-4pm Sat & Sun*), which crafts chocolates from Peruvian cacao. Staff members allow visitors to taste-test treats before buying; try the plummy Morropon.

Say '*santé*' to HoMa at microbrewery **L'Espace Public** (*lespacepublic.ca; hours vary Wed-Sun*), where communal picnic tables overflow onto a seasonal terrace. Sours are the specialty.

 TOUR CHÂTEAU DUFRESNE

Nothing inspires real-estate envy like visiting this **beaux-arts mansion** (MAP: ④ P75 **F2**; *chateaudufresne.com; adult/child $14/7*) facing Parc Olympique. Constructed from 1915 to 1918, the château was modeled after the Petit Trianon in Versailles and decked out with interiors fit for a king: parquet floors, stained-glass windows and coffered ceilings with frescoes by Italian artist Guido Nincheri. Half the home is largely empty, allowing visitors to focus on architectural elements and frescoes (look up in the living room to see 15 paintings depicting Orpheus and Eurydice). The other half is furnished with early 20th century decor. The Château is closed Mondays and Tuesdays.

LISTINGS

Best Places for...

$** Budget **$$** Midrange **$$$ Top End

Eating

Fab Food Cafes

Le Café Big Trouble $$
6 A3
This colorfully off-kilter brunch-and-coffee counter on Rue St-Denis recalls the street's hip heydays. Try the loaded breakfast burrito or fluffy pancakes. *@lecafebigtrouble, 8am-4pm Thu-Sun*

La Graine Brûlée $
7 C5
If an eight-year-old from 1995 opened a vegetarian coffeehouse, this would be it – vintage video-game den, excessive carnival decor, bagel sandwiches and all. *ouimanon.com, 7am-10pm*

Café Sfouf $
8 E2
Settle into this boho hang with the work-from-anywhere crowd for *tartines* (toasts) topped with Lebanese flavors (labneh, za'atar, pistachio). *@cafesfouf, 8am-6pm Tue-Fri, 8:30am-5pm Sat & Sun*

Dinner in the Village

Le Red Tiger $
9 E4
Sidle up to the canary-yellow bar for Vietnamese street food like deep-fried pancakes and crunchy imperial rolls. *leredtiger.com, 5-10pm Mon-Thu, to 11pm Fri & Sat*

Othym $$$
10 D5
Menus change weekly at this minimalist outpost for epicurious omnivores. Expect game and greens sourced from Québec farms. BYO wine. *othym.com, 5:30-10pm*

Bars & Pubs with Grub

Marion Tavern $$
11 D2
This light, bright corner cocktail bar serves flatbreads and artisanal beers later than most – a fantastic 'last call' in the Village. *tavernemarion, 4pm-3am*

Blossom $$
12 D4
Lounge beneath cherry blossoms and choose from an extensive list of sakes and makis inside this glass-walled, neo-Japanese joint. *leblossom.ca, 5-10pm Tue-Thu, to 10:30pm Fri & Sat*

Drinking

Craft Beer & Blues

Le Cheval Blanc
13 C3
Raise a glass to Montréal's first microbrewery, pouring homemade craft since the 1980s. The digs might seem dingy, but the suds remain stellar and there's occasionally live music. *lechevalblanc.ca, 3pm-3am Tues-Sat, to 1am Sun & Mon*

Brasseurs du Monde
14 B4
This two-story spot takes *'l'art de la bière'* seriously, as a tap-side sign suggests. Try a four-beer flight, locally made.

brasseursdumonde.com, 1am-1am Mon-Fri, from 10am Sat & Sun

Bistro à Jojo
 B4

Booze, blues and rock 'n' roll: get it all at this Rue St-Denis venue, jamming to live tunes since 1975. *bistroajojo.com, noon-3am*

Rue Ste-Catherine's LGBTIQ+ Bars

Renard
 E5

This 'Fox' has a split personality: weeknights he's a 5 à 7 cocktail-with-dinner gentleman; weekends he's a dance-till-dawn diva. *bar-renard.com, 3pm-1am Sun-Wed, to 3am Thu-Sat*

Aigle Noir
 E5

Four bars, three floors, and a series of slot machines where you might see leather-clad bears gambling for a lucky night: shoot your shot. *aiglenoir.ca, 8am-3am*

Stud
 H5

It's a veritable zoo at this 'men's bar', its two dance floors packed with leather bears, pool sharks, furry pups and, occasionally, fresh-faced bucks. *lestudmontreal.com, 2pm-3am*

Saloon
 F5

This queer-centric alternative to dance dens serves dinner until 8pm before doubling down on cocktails. *lesaloon.ca, 5pm-midnight Sun-Thu, to 1:30am Fri & Sat*

Dance Dens

Stereo
 C5

Melodic house and transcendental techno flood the speakers of this all-hours dance floor, revered by Montréal club kids for its exceptional sound system. *tixr.com/groups/stereo, midnight-9am Fri & Sat*

Motel Motel
 E5

Pass the tiny cocktail lounge up front to reach the cozy dance floor hidden in the back, its LED ceiling glowing like a Lite-Brite board on acid. *@motel_motel_, 9pm-3am Fri & Sat*

Turbo Haüs
 A3

Up-and-coming bands play to petite crowds in this lower-level bar and music venue known for rocking punk and metal music, along with open-mic nights on Tuesdays. *turbohaus.ca, 5pm-midnight Sun-Wed, to 3am Thu-Sat*

Shopping

Maps, Cheese & Teas

Aux Quatre Points Cardinaux
 C3

Find your way with this encyclopedic assortment of maps, globes, atlases, aerial photographs and a commendable collection of Lonely Planet guides. *aqpc.com, 10am-5pm Mon-Wed & Sat, to 7pm Thu & Fri*

Fromagerie Atwater
 E2

Prep a charcuterie board with a superb selection of meats and cheeses. Opt for a local *fromage* such as the Bête-à-Séguin, a camembert from Isle-aux-Grues on the St Lawrence River. *fromagerieatwater.ca, 9am-7pm Mon-Fri, to 6pm Sat & Sun*

Camellia Sinensis
 A4

Order an oolong to go, peruse the white canisters of loose leaf or grab a seat to compare your favorites with a tea tasting ($5 per cup). *camellia-sinensis.com, 11am-6pm Mon-Sat, from noon Sun*

See p97 for eating, drinking and shopping listings

Explore
Plateau Mont-Royal

Researched by
John Garry

Splashed in street art, brimming with boutiques and bookended by gorgeous green spaces, the 'Plateau' is home to some of the city's most sought-after real estate. Since the 19th century, it has evolved from a mix of bourgeois families in graystones and working-class immigrants in multiplexes to a center for Jewish life, an outpost for Portuguese immigrants, and most recently, a magnet for newcomers from France. Blvd St-Laurent (dubbed the Main) runs north–south through it all, historically dividing English and French speakers. These days, it's the hip heart of the neighborhood, forming a mosaic of Montréal's arty, international spirit.

Getting Around

 Métro
Take the orange line to Sherbrooke (south) or Mont-Royal (north) along Rue Berri.

 Bus
Bus 55 travels along Blvd St-Laurent; bus 30 runs along Rue St-Denis; bus 80 follows Ave du Parc; bus 11 chugs along Ave Mont-Royal and up Parc du Mont-Royal (until 2027 when the road is replaced by a walking path).

 **Walk & Bicycle**
For walking, Blvd St-Laurent and Rue St-Denis are the neighborhood's most energetic north–south thoroughfares. Aves Mont-Royal and Duluth are best for traveling east–west. For cycling, follow protected bike lanes along Rue St-Denis and Rue Rachel.

THE BEST

STREET ART
See magnificent murals (p92)

FANTASTIC VIEWS
Belvédère Kondiaronk (p90)

TASTY SANDWICHES
Schwartz's (p94)

PEDESTRIAN PROMENADE
Ave Duluth (p95)

LOCAL ART SHOP
L'Original (p99)

Parc La Fontaine (p94)
EDUARDO FONSECA ARRAES/GETTY IMAGES

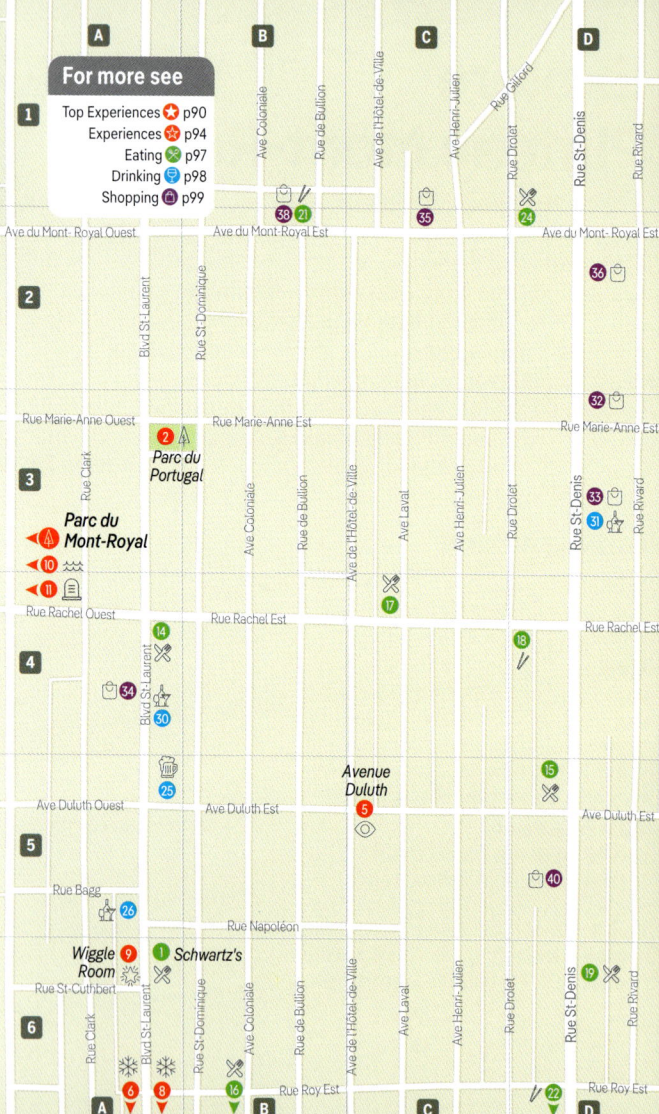

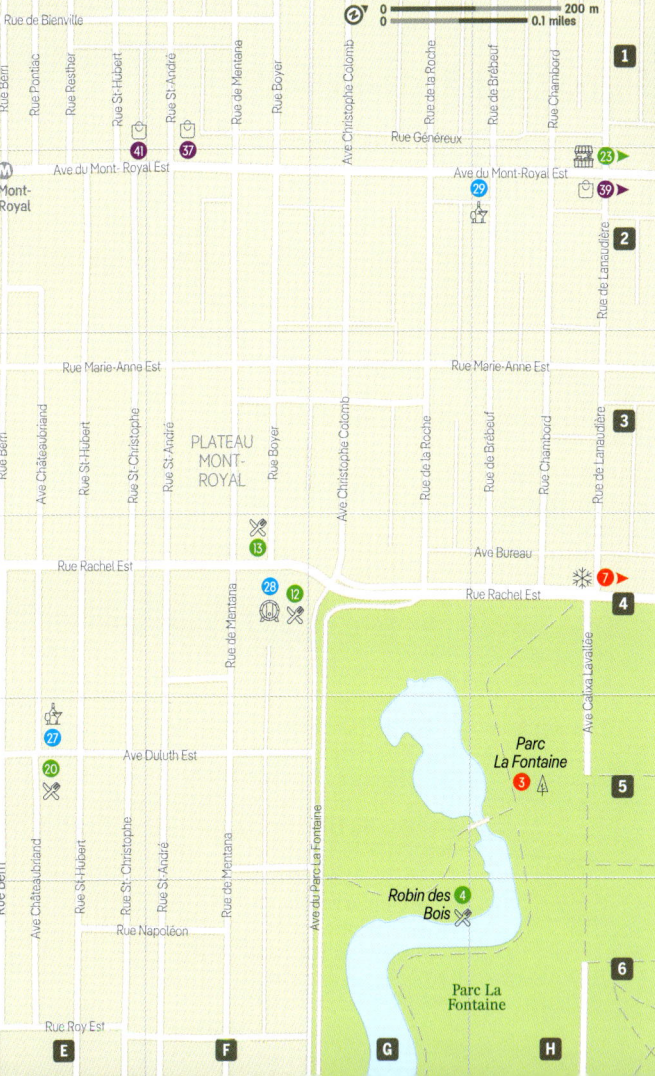

★ **TOP EXPERIENCE**

Parc du Mont-Royal

Inaugurated in 1876 and designed by green space guru Frederick Law Olmsted (of New York City's Central Park fame), **Parc du Mont-Royal** is a 280-hectare symphony of woodlands, meadows and winding trails. It covers Montréal's noble 'Mountain' – as locals call it – rising 233m above sea level and majestic year-round.

MAP P88 **A3**

PLANNING TIP
To see the major sites, follow Chemin Olmsted, a 4.4km trail snaking from the **Cartier Monument** to Beaver Lake and arriving at **Belvédère Kondiaronk**, the park's exclamation point.

Scan this QR code for the latest park info and hours.

Spectacular Sites

The park's loveliest viewpoint is **Belvédère Kondiaronk**, a terrace overlooking Downtown's skyscrapers. It's connected to **Chalet du Mont-Royal**, a beaux-arts lodge from 1932 with a cafe, gift shop, bathrooms and information kiosk. The cavernous chalet features canvases by 13 Canadian artists depicting Montréal's history. Look up: 32 wood-carved, nut-clutching squirrels lurk in the rafters.

Belvédère Camillien-Houde showcases a panorama dominated by the angled Montréal Tower. During 2027 the roadway here is set to become a pedestrian path.

Lac aux Castors (p96; Beaver Lake) is the park's recreational epicenter. From late June to September, it's all about rowboating. Winter sports rule from December to March. Stop by the **Pavillon du Lac aux Castors** along the lake's northwestern banks to rent outdoor gear and games. End your excursion with the après-sport crowd in the pavilion's top-floor cafe *(9am-6pm)* for snacks and drinks, served year-round.

Maison Smith, headquarters for Les Amis de la Montagne, hosts an exhibition on Mont Royal's ecology. A cafe sells grilled sandwiches, soups,

HICHAM EL ASRI/SHUTTERSTOCK

desserts and drinks; a gift shop hawks bird-watching paraphernalia and souvenirs.

Major Monuments

On warm-weather Sundays, the bronze-and-granite **Sir Georges-Étienne Cartier Monument**, soaring above the Plateau, vibrates to the beat of **Tam-Tams du Mont-Royal** – a free, informal event where diverse crowds groove to a cacophonous chorus of tam-tams (bongo-style drums).

The 33m-tall **Croix du Mont-Royal**, a skyline icon raised in 1924, commemorates the spot where Montréal founder Paul de Chomedey (p44) carried a wooden cross in 1643 to thank the Virgin Mary for saving the city from flood.

QUICK BREAK
Pause for drinks and light meals at the cafes in **Chalet du Mont-Royal** (10am-6pm Mon-Fri, to 8pm Sat & Sun; $), **Maison Smith** and **Pavillon du Lac aux Castors** (9am-6pm, $).

WALKING TOUR

See Magnificent Murals

Montréal is covered in kaleidoscopic street art. Early June's **MURAL Festival** *(muralfestival.com)* sees international wall-scrawlers make their mark around Plateau's Blvd St-Laurent. To see the most recent artwork, join an expert tour with **Spade & Palacio** *(spadeandpalacio.com)* or scour the streets alone.

START	END	LENGTH
Corner of Rues St-Dominique and Napoléon	53 Rue Milton	1.6km; 1 hr

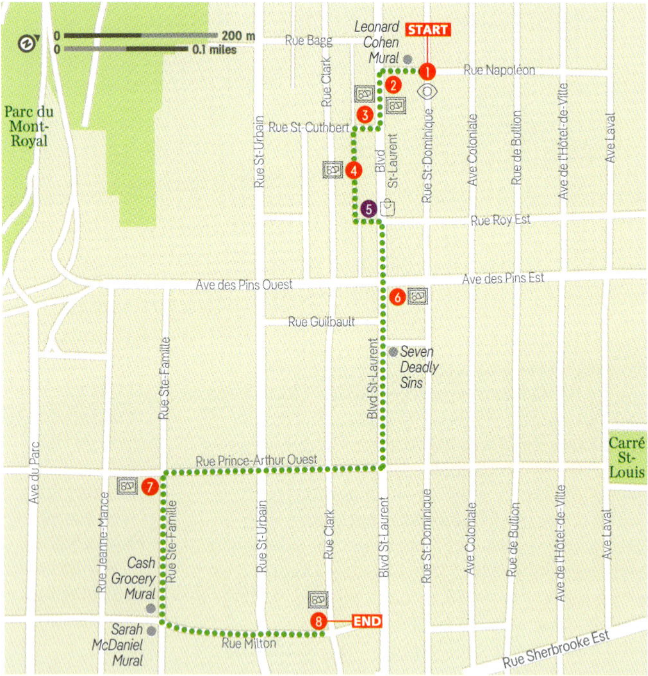

1 Plateau Poet
Look up on the **corner of Rues St-Dominique and Napoléon** to see singer-songwriter Leonard Cohen's two-story eyes (Kevin Ledo) watching over the neighborhood where he spent the latter half of his life.

2 Technicolor History
En route to Blvd St-Laurent, find the photorealistic **portrait of Jackie Robinson** who played minor league baseball in Montréal before breaking the US major league color barrier in 1947. Artist Fluke used brooms to create the colorful swaths of paint overlaying Robinson's likeness.

3 Legendary Muralist
At 3860 Blvd St-Laurent Montréal artists Axe Lalime and Zek One preserved **Karma goID**, the work of beloved local graffiti legend Scaner, who passed away in 2017. Spot the gold clover, Montréal's official symbol, on the right-hand side.

4 Tiny Installations
Continue down the alley off St-Laurent, perpendicular to Rue St-Cuthbert, with a rotating **graffiti collection**, and make a left to reach Rue Roy. Before exiting the alley, look up near the A&W sign: a miniature man in boxer shorts, clandestinely placed by Spanish artist Isaac Cordal. Keep your eyes peeled – more of Cordal's mini men hide around the Plateau.

5 Street Style
Cut back to Blvd St-Laurent along Rue Roy to peer inside **Artgang** *(artgangmontreal.com)* a boutique selling streetwear like sneakers and tees. The Artgang crew also produces murals throughout the city. Prints and originals of their work can be found inside.

6 Graffiti Granny
Back on the street, continue south past 3725 Blvd St-Laurent to greet the Plateau's gray-haired mascot, a **graffiti-loving grandma** (by street-art team TYXNA), then take in *Seven Deadly Sins* (Buff Monster) on the wall of hot dog and burger joint Dirty Dogs *(dirty-dogs.shop)*.

7 Beautiful Bodies
Veer west on Rue Prince Arthur to 3598 Rue St-Famille to see **Personal Topography** (Klone Yourself, 2016) – a reflection on the way bodies collect experiences like tree trunk rings – then bop one block south, where the heterochromatic eyes of Sarah McDaniel (Drew Merrit, 2017) look toward Cash Grocery (Matéo, 2016).

8 Art as Protest
Finish strong at 53 Rue Milton's **La liberté vandalisée** (*Freedom Vandalized*; Escif, 2024), a contemporary take on Eugène Delacroix's revolutionary-themed painting *La liberté guidant le peuple* (1830). The work is layered with defiant graffiti tags by local artists.

EXPERIENCES

Savor a Sandwich at Schwartz's

SMOKED MEAT

MAP: ① P88 **A6**

Eating smoked meat is a Montréal must and **Schwartz's** (*schwartzsdeli.com; 10am-11pm Sun-Thu, to midnight Fri & Sat; $*) is the best place to try it. The meat has been made the same way since 1928, when Romanian Jewish immigrant Reuben Schwartz opened this shop. It's cured for 10 days, smoked overnight and sliced by hand to order – and crowds can't get enough. Some diners go for the rib steak and poutine, but the juicy brisket sandwich is best, stacked higher than Mont Royal between two pieces of mustard-slathered rye bread. Prepare to wait in line for the sit-down experience, or save time by ordering yours to go from the deli next door, where you'll find a counter and some tables in back.

Tour Petit Portugal

MEALS AND MONUMENTS

MAP: ② P88 **A3**

Over 50,000 people in the greater Montréal area have Portuguese roots – many connected to immigrants who settled in the Plateau throughout the 1950s and '60s. Their impact is most evident along a stretch of Blvd St-Laurent from Ave des Pins to Rue Marie-Anne, dubbed Petit Portugal.

Start by admiring the *azulejo* (glazed tile)–adorned entrance of **Parc du Portugal**, with a monument dedicated to the neighborhood's first Portuguese residents. Continue south to **Les Anges Gourmets** (*7am-4pm Tue-Sat; $*) for *pastel de nata* (custard tarts), best when sprinkled with cinnamon. Switch to savory at **Coco Rico** (*10am-9pm Sun-Wed, to 10pm Thu-Sat; $*), founded in 1970 and considered the city's first outpost for Portuguese-style rôtisserie chicken, now a Montréal cuisine staple. The counter serves its birds with *piripiri* (Swahili for 'pepper pepper'), a fiery sauce inspired by Portuguese-African cooking. Get yours on a sandwich to scarf down counterside.

Hang Out in Parc La Fontaine

OUTDOOR RECREATION

Stretching 40 hectares across the Plateau, **Parc La Fontaine** (MAP: ③ P89 **H5**) is the city's eastern answer to Parc du Mont-Royal, ideal for summer strolling and winter snowshoeing around its two waterfall-linked ponds.

In warm months, folks flock to its green fields, perimeter bike paths and **Théâtre de Verdure** (*montreal.ca/lieux/theatre-de-verdure*), an outdoor amphitheater with free programming from late June through August. Check the schedule for performances.

When winter blows in, ice skaters take to the frozen pond and cross-country skiers glide along

5.2km of groomed trails. **Patin Patin** (patinpatin.ca) offers skate and ski rentals inside the park chalet, running from mid-January to early March.

The chalet doubles as the restaurant and event space for **Robin des Bois** (MAP: ④ P89 **G6**; robindesbois.ca; 10am-5pm Wed & Sun, to 10pm Thu-Sat; $), where you can drop in for sandwiches, soups, coffee and beer – and possibly catch a live jazz set or drag brunch, all listed on the website's calendar.

Dip Down Ave Duluth
PEDESTRIAN THOROUGHFARE

MAP: ⑤ P88 **C5**

From mid-May to mid-October, **Ave Duluth** (avenueduluth.ca) closes to cars between Blvd St-Laurent and Rue St-Hubert. Join pedestrians on this 750m brick-paved stretch by stopping in boutiques, imbibing on streetside terraces and admiring murals decorating its buildings.

For shopping, flip through lit at English-language bookstore **De Stiil** (destiil.com), then step inside **Le Magasin Général Lambert Gratton** (@magasingenerallambertgratton) to find everything from vintage kitchenware and old-school candies to Montréal-inspired print art. If you've got kids in tow, peek inside **La Grande Ourse** (boutiquelagrandeourse.ca), an old-world treasure chest that shirks iPad playtime for nontoxic toys crafted by local makers. Finish with a sugar fix at **Les Chocolats de Chloé** (leschocolatsdechloe.com), a primary-colored chocolate truffle shop where each square morsel gets made in-house.

There's often a free alfresco weekend concert to attend (usually between noon and 8pm), plus several weeklong festivals highlighting local gastronomy gurus such as microbrewers and cheese-makers. Check the avenue's official website for programming details.

ICE RINKS WITH SKATE RENTALS

Atrium Le 1000
MAP: ⑥ P88 **A6**
Hop on the ice year-round at this glass-domed indoor rink, located on the ground floor of 1000 De la Gauchetière, dominating Downtown's skyline. (le1000.com/fr)

Parc Maisonneuve
MAP: ⑦ P89 **H4**
Ring around the icy outdoor oval in this HoMa park shadowed by the Olympic Stadium's Montréal Tower.

Esplanade Tranquille
MAP: ⑧ P88 **A6**
The city's largest refrigerated rink covers 1500 sq meters in the heart of Downtown's Quartier des Spectacles from mid-November to early April. Video projections illuminate the ice at night.

Giggle at the Wiggle Room
BURLESQUE

MAP: **9** P88 **A6**

Montréal's **Wiggle Room** *(wiggle room.ca; tickets from $37)* is Canada's only full-time burlesque cabaret – and one of the few woman-owned burlesque businesses in North America. Frenchy Jones presides over the pasty party with aplomb, bringing a feminist point of view to an art form historically designed for the male gaze. In addition to feather-boa femmes, shows here may include gender-bending boylesque, drag, stand-up and live music. There's a ragtag quality to each performance – from the itty-bitty stage to the tassel-twirling talent, which runs the gamut from basic to brilliant.

Shows run Wednesday to Sunday, starting at 8pm. Arrive early to choose your seat – the bar opens at 7pm. Themed shows take place throughout the week – check the schedule to see what's on.

Explore Mountain Mausoleums
MONT ROYAL CEMETERIES

Over a million permanent residents occupy the necropolis north of Parc du Mont-Royal, spread among a series of serene, free-to-visit cemeteries – ideal for some solemn strolling.

You can pay your respects to roughly 900,000 souls – including former mayor Jean Drapeau – rest north of the park's **Lac aux Castors** (MAP: **10** P88 **A3**) inside the 139-hectare **Cimetière Notre-Dame-des-Neiges** (MAP: **11** P88 **A4**; *cimetierenotredamedesneiges.ca*), Canada's largest cemetery, established in 1854 and inspired by the Père-Lachaise in Paris.

East of here – and north of Parc du Mont Royal's **Maison Smith** (p90) – lies **Cimetière Mont-Royal** *(mountroyalcem.com)*, founded in 1852. Its terraced grounds slope over 67 hectares covered in century-old trees and granite headstones serenaded by over 100 bird species. Some 200,000 people lay buried beneath it all, including Montréal author Mordecai Richler.

Shaar Hashomayim Cemetery *(shaarhashomayim.org/cemetery)*, established by Montréal's Ashkenazi Jewish community in 1863, sits just east of Cimetière Mont-Royal. Enter on Blvd de la Forêt to find folk star Leonard Cohen's grave, then cue up his haunting 'Hallelujah', a musical poem about faith, love and loss.

LISTINGS

Best Places for...

$ Budget $$ Midrange $$$ Top End

See p88 for map of locations

Eating

Plates of Poutine

La Banquise $
⑫ F4
Choose from over 30 cheese curd concoctions at this *poutinerie*, perfected since the 1980s. Carnivores: come for the T-rex, topped with ground beef, pepperoni, bacon and sausage. Expect weekend wait times. *labanquise.com, 24hr*

Ma Poule Mouillée $
⑬ F4
It's Québec poutine sprinkled with Azores flavors: tangy São Jorge cheese, chicken and chorizo, all glazed in a special garlicky sauce. Grab yours to go and nosh in Parc La Fontaine. *mapoulemouillee.ca, 10am-9pm Tue-Sun*

Patati Patata $
⑭ A4
Get the breakfast poutine (eggs, bacon and sausage), crowned with a signature olive, at this diner – slimmer than a French fry and open since 1996. *patatimontreal.ca, 11am-2am*

International Lunch Fare

La Panzeria $$
⑮ D5
Take a trip to Puglia inside this St-Denis cafe by ordering a deep-fried, cheese-stuffed *panzerotti* (dough pocket), followed by a pillowy *bombolone* (a cream-crammed doughnut). *lapanzeria.com, hours vary*

Arepera $$
⑯ B6
Pews line the entrance to this restaurant praising Venezuelan *arepas* (meat, cheese and veggie-stuffed corn cakes). *arepera.ca, 11:30am-9pm Tue-Sat, 10am-3pm Sun*

Cafe Chez Téta $
⑰ C4
Manouche (Lebanese flatbreads) accompany cardamom coffee and chunky pistachio halva lattes. *cafechezteta.com, 9am-7:30pm Wed-Fri, to 5pm Sat & Sun*

Yokato Yokabai $$
⑱ D4
Warm up during Montréal's coldest days with a steaming bowl of pork-based *tonkotsu* ramen accompanied by handmade noodles. *yoka.ca, hours vary*

French & Québécois Classics

L'Express $$$
⑲ D6
'Left Bank bistro' serving this side of the Atlantic since 1980 – beef tartare, brisk waiters, black-and-white tiles and all. Reservations recommended for dinner and weekend brunch. *restaurantlexpress.com, 11:30am-2am*

Au Pied de Cochon $$$
⑳ E5
Meat in a can. Meat on poutine. Meat in dessert. Foie-gras essence in cocktails. It's fatty, decadent and quintessentially Québécois. *aupieddecochon.ca, 5-11pm Wed-Sun*

Japanese Influence

Kitano Shokudo $$$
 B2

Fish, Japan-imported or Québec-caught, stars in *chirashi* bowls at this seasonally attuned Japanese joint. *bistrootto.com, 11:30am-1:30pm & 5:30-8:30pm Mon, Tue, Thu & Fri*

Momo $$
22 D6

Vegan sushi rolls? More like avant-garde flavor bombs with styles ranging from funky cheese to garden fresh, all elevating Japanese tradition. *sushimomo.ca, hours vary*

Delicious Delis & Baked Goods

Bleu & Persillé $
23 H2

Find your favorite Québec cheese and pair it with other local products sold on-site, such as Qantu chocolate and Miel honey test tubes. *bleuetpersille.ca, 11am-7pm Tue, 10pm-7pm Wed-Sat, 11am-6pm Sun*

Le Toledo $
24 D2

French pastries (cakes, eclairs, quiches, croissants) are prepared with local ingredients by an army of bakers, visible through glass windows. Try the apple-stuffed *chausson aux pommes*. *letoledo.com, 7am-6pm*

Drinking

Craft Beer & Barcade

Réservoir
25 A5

Beers come with bite at this warmly lit, two-floor brewery featuring a summer deck overlooking Duluth. Try the sour candy–flavored Mont Royal. *brasseriereservoir.com, hours vary*

North Star Machines
26 A5

Become a pinball wizard while slamming flippers (the controls on a pinball machine) and downing beers inside this second-floor 'bar-cade' with a retro photo booth. *northstarpinball.com, 5pm-1am Sun, Mon, Wed & Thu, to 3am Fri & Sat*

Wine & Whiskey

Bar Vivar
 E5

Score bar seats to watch chefs prep Spanish tapas (tortillas, croquettes) while sipping old-world wines. @restaurantbarvivar, 11:30am-9pm Wed-Fri, 10am-9pm Sat, to 4pm Sun

Projet Pilote
28 F4

A spiral staircase ascends to 2nd-floor tanks where the magic is made in this soaring-ceiling distillery with occasional live music. *projetpilote.com, 5pm-1am*

Le Rouge-Gorge
29 H2

Grab a two-top table to sample wines inside this upscale, unstuffy bar guarded by a tiny *rouge-gorge* (robin). *rougegorge.ca, 3pm-midnight Sun-Tue, to 1am Wed-Sat*

Cocktails & Live Music

Majestique
30 A4

The decor (vintage globes, jeroboams, a mascot bunny bead) are as eclectic as the cocktail list and fish-forward tapas menu. Come for the 5 à 7 oyster special. *restobarmajestique.com, 4pm-3am*

Big in Japan
  D3

A bow-tied waiter takes orders behind the labyrinthine bar, swirling like a dragon's tail in this sexy, unmarked speakeasy beside Patati Patata. @biginjapan_bar, 5pm-3am

Shopping

Upcycled Fashion

Cafe Camas
32 D3

Leather couches up front, funky sweaters in back and a coffee counter in between: stop here for a pick-me-up while shopping along Rue St-Denis. *@cafe.camas, 8am-6pm Mon-Fri, from 9am Sat & Sun*

Marché Floh
33 D3

Wander through three floors crammed with thrifty finds, separated by punk-rock attire (basement), masc streetwear (ground floor) and femme flair (upstairs). *marchefloh.com, noon-9pm Mon-Fri, 11am-6pm Sat & Sun*

Quality Vintage

La Caravane Vintage
34 A4

Owner Erika Devile has been restoring vintage denim, leather and plaid since 2019, all sold from this pretty Blvd St-Laurent shop. *lacaravanevintage.com, 11am-6pm Mon-Wed & Sat, to 7pm Thu & Fri, to 5pm Sun*

Palmo Goods
35 C2

This small, handpicked selection of quality vintage roots itself in collegiate, military and Americana styles with options ranging from affordable to top dollar. *palmogoods.com, noon-6pm Mon-Fri, from 11am Sat, noon-5pm Sun*

Street Art Styles

L'Original
36 D2

Local muralists sell canvases, some at affordable prices, inside this two-floor gallery with paint-splashed studios upstairs. There's a second gallery location in Old Montréal. *loriginal.org, 11am-6pm, Mon-Fri, to 6:30pm Sat & Sun*

Le Cartel
37 F2

Savvy streetwear serves as canvases for muralists, photographers and graphic designers at this clothing brand and art collective. Styles change every few months. *lecartelclothing.com, 10am-8pm*

Local Art & Souvenirs

Artpop
38 B2

Around 80 creatives fill this small shop with quirky souvenirs such as poutine magnets, CBC-branded socks and postcards of street art. *artpopmontreal.com, 11am-7pm Sun-Fri, from 10am Sat*

Affiche en Tête
39 H2

Pick out affordable local art, such as Sébastien Beaupré's Montréal-themed photographs and André-Anne Guay's Québec-inspired collages, at this frame-and-prints purveyor. *afficheentete.ca, 10am-6pm Mon-Fri, to 5pm Sat, noon-5pm Sun*

Livart
40 D5

Once a presbytery, these holy halls on Rue St-Denis now house contemporary art galleries, artist studios and a colorful shop selling books, paintings and prints. *lelivart.com, noon-6pm Thu & Fri, 11am-5pm Sat & Sun*

Multimags
41 E2

Flip through hard-to-find design magazines in English and French, pick up the *Montréal Gazette* or pick out a coffee-table Taschen tome inside the Ave Mont-Royal location of this chain. *pressecommercecorp.com, 9am-9pm*

Explore
Mile End, Little Italy & Outremont

Researched by
John Garry

Immigrants and artists spent the last century transforming these neighborhoods into epicenters for foodies and fashionistas. Mile End, an industrial 20th-century manufacturing district and Jewish hub, was once a 'mile' from the city's northern border. Today it's the cusp of Montréal cool, crammed with restaurants, boutiques and murals. Little Italy, located on the western side of the Petite-Patrie borough, started waving its namesake nation's flag in the early 1900s. The neighborhood's culinary heritage now blends European, Latin American, Asian and Middle Eastern influences. Outremont moves from mansions lining Parc du Mont-Royal, home to wealthy francophones, to brick multiplexes belonging to a Hasidic stronghold.

Getting Around

 Métro
Take the orange line to Laurier for Mile End. Ride the orange or blue lines to Jean-Talon for Little Italy. Outremont has its own station on the blue line.

 Bus
Bus 55 runs north–south along Blvd St-Laurent through Mile End and Little Italy; bus 46 zigzags through Mile End and Outremont; bus 80 runs along Ave du Parc, linking Outremont to Downtown and beyond.

 Walk
Blvd St-Laurent is the main artery connecting Mile End and Little Italy.

THE BEST

VIBRANT FOOD MARKET
Marché Jean-Talon (p110)

OLD-SCHOOL BAKERY
Fairmount Bagel (p108)

UPSCALE BISTRO
Vin Mon Lapin (p111)

INDIE MUSIC
Casa del Popolo (p109)

PEACEFUL PARK
Île de la Visitation (p104)

Marché Jean-Talon (p110)
KRISTI BLOKHIN/SHUTTERSTOCK

MILE END, LITTLE ITALY & OUTREMONT

EXPLORE

Points of interest (from map)

- Île de la Visitation
- Marché Jean-Talon
- Caffè Italia
- Parc de la Petite-Italie

Streets referenced

- Rue Jean-Talon Est / Ouest
- Rue de Normanville
- Rue Chambord
- Rue de la Roche
- Rue St-Zotique Est
- Rue Beaubien Est
- Rue de Bellechasse
- Ave Christophe-Colomb
- Rue St-André
- Rue Boyer
- Rue Bélanger
- Rue St-Hubert
- Ave de Chateaubriand
- Rue Le St-Vallier
- Beaubien
- Rue St-Denis
- Rue Drolet
- Ave Henri-Julien
- Rue Alma
- Ave de Gaspé
- Ave Casgrain
- Rue St-Dominique
- Blvd St-Laurent
- Rue Clark
- Rue St-Urbain
- Ave Mozart Est / Ouest
- Rue Dante
- Ave Beaumont
- Rue de Castelnau Ouest / Est
- De Castelnau
- Rue Waverly
- Rue Alexandra
- Rue Marconi
- Rue St-Zotique Ouest
- Ave de l'Esplanade
- Rue Jeanne-Mance
- Rue Beaubien Ouest
- Ave du Parc
- Rue Hutchison
- Rue Durocher
- Ave Querbes
- Ave de l'Épée
- Ave Bloomfield
- Ave Champagneur
- Ave d'Outremont
- Ave Ogilvy
- Ave Van Horne
- Ave Ducharme
- Outremont

102

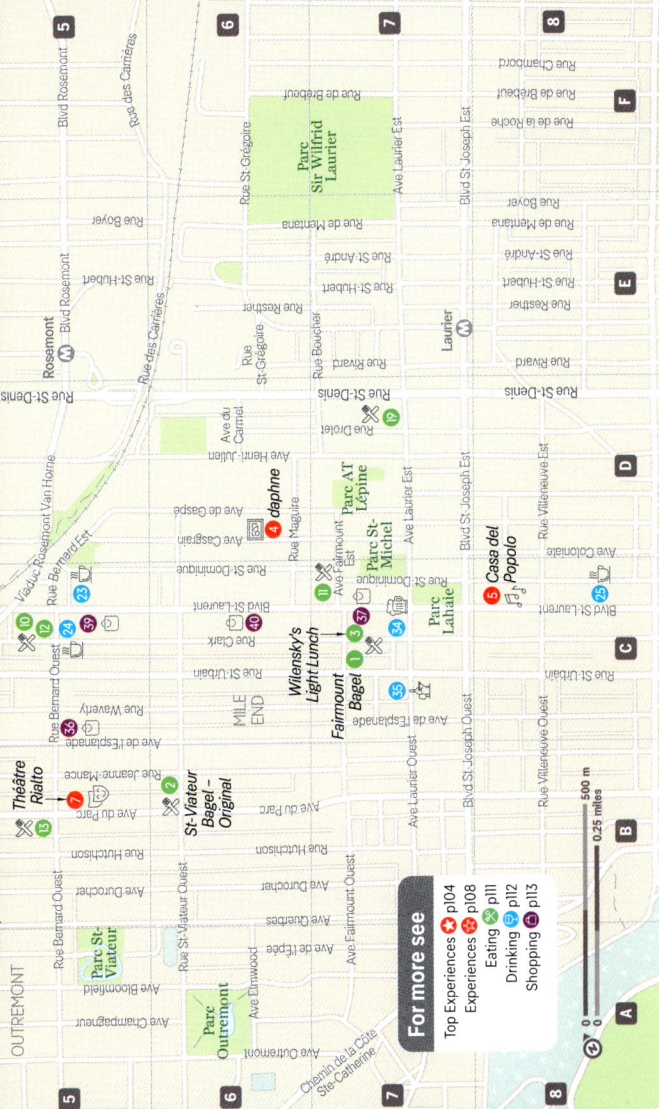

★ TOP EXPERIENCE

Cycle to Île de la Visitation

Pedal to Montréal's north side for a peaceful afternoon along the Rivière des Prairies – or as the Kanien'kehá:ka (Mohawk) aptly named it, the 'River Behind the Island.' Along this urban waterway sits the **Parc-nature de l'Île-de-la-Visitation**, a pretty 34-hectare green space rooted around industrial ruins.

MAP P102 **C1**

PLANNING TIP
The bike ride here covers roughly 11km one way. Budget for three hours or more and enjoy a waterfront picnic. Plan your trip between snow-free spring and autumn.

Scan the QR code for park hours and services.

Cycling Route

Rent a bicycle from **Fitz Montréal** (*fitzmontreal.com; 10am-5pm/24hr $45/55*), near Parc La Fontaine. Follow Rue Rachel west to St-Denis, where a protected REV lane (part of MTL's express cycling network, 'Réseau Express Vélo') speeds north to Little Italy. Pause for coffee at **Zab**, located along the bike path on St-Denis, or take a quick detour to **Marché Jean-Talon** (p110) to stack up on picnic supplies.

Navigate to Ave Christophe Colomb and go north until it dead-ends at Blvd Gouin. Follow Blvd Gouin east to the park, passing Victorian houses with grassy lawns – a sure sign urban Montréal is miles away. Look out for **Église La Visitation-de-la-Bienheureuse-Vierge-Marie** (Church of the Visitation of the Blessed Virgin Mary). One of the city's oldest churches, initially completed in 1752, its two steeple-topped towers shine silver above Blvd Gouin.

At the Park

Lock your bike on racks beside **Le Festigoût Cafe** (*10am-5pm Sat & Sun; $*), selling soup and sandwiches from a stone house with a scenic terrace overlooking the water. Tree-trimmed

AWANA JF/SHUTTERSTOCK

footpaths stretch along the water lapping Montréal's mainland and Île de la Visitation, the bridge-connected island, where turtles sun on rocks and birds flit among the branches. It's a great spot for a picnic lunch.

From Industrial Site to Green Space
Between mainland Montréal and Île-de-la-Visitation rush the Sault-au-Récollet rapids. In 1726, the Sulpicians (a society of Catholic missionaries) erected a mill above the waterway to harness the hydraulic energy of the rapids – the first of several buildings that would go on to produce items like wheat, wool, nails and paper until the mid-20th century. In 1998, the area was transformed into a park. Only the vine-choked foundations of the industrial site remain.

TAKE A BREAK
Stop by **Racer Cafe de Course** *(hours vary; $)*, a Blvd Gouin bike cafe near the park's entrance serving coffee, protein-packed snacks and ice cream.

WALKING TOUR

Jump into Jewish History

The Plateau and Mile End served as epicenters for Montréal's Jewish community, tens of thousands strong, from 1900 to 1950. By the 1960s, Jewish families started leaving for the western suburbs and beyond, but their mark remains in beloved bakeries, luncheonettes and religious architecture.

START	END	LENGTH
Bagg Street Shul	Musée du Montréal Juif	3km; 2 hrs

1 House of Worship

Bagg Street Shul, Québec's oldest functioning synagogue, is the sole survivor of roughly two dozen Jewish houses of worship that once graced the neighborhood. Originally a two-family complex built in 1889, it was converted into a synagogue in 1921.

2 Meeting Spot

Skirt past Parc Jeanne-Mance, once known as **Fletcher's Field** – a 20th-century gathering place for Jewish families near the entrance to Parc du Mont-Royal. The Croix du Mont-Royal overlooks the scene, an omnipresent reminder of the city's Catholic dominance.

3 Classic Eats

Head east on Ave Mont-Royal to see the sepia-tone mural of Hymie and Freda Sckolnick, who opened **Beautys** (*beautys.ca; 8am-3pm Mon & Wed-Fri, to 4pm Sat & Sun*) in 1942. Beauty was Hymie's bowling nickname and the Sckolnicks' descendants still greet guests at the door of this classic diner.

4 Pastries with Chutzpah

Save your appetite for Jewish-French fusion bakery **Hof Kelsten** (*hofkelsten.com; 8am-5pm*), run by chef Jeffrey Finkelstein since 2013, and order the *croissant tout-garni*. This everything-seasoned, cream cheese-stuffed treat nods at Montréal's Jewish-born bagel culture. Come on Friday to score a shiny loaf of challah – right on time for the Sabbath.

5 Montréal Mensch

Move into Mile End toward 25 Ave Laurier, past a **mural of Montréal author Mordecai Richler** (1931—2001), who wrote vividly about the Jewish experience in this neighborhood. (Richler grew up nearby on Rue St-Urbain). Richler's most famous novel, *The Apprenticeship of Duddy Kravitz*, captures working-class Mile End and posh Outremont in the 1940s and '50s.

6 Architectural Remnant

Stroll north along Ave Esplanada to Collège Français. Peer above the Pavilion Montaigne on Ave Fairmount to spot the grand, ghostly arch of a defunct synagogue, **B'Nai Jacob** (1918), still visible above the new structure.

7 Neighborhood Nosh

Jog back toward Blvd St-Laurent, passing Jewish food favorites **Fairmount Bagel** (p108) and **Wilensky's Light Lunch** (p108). Order the Wilensky Special (bologna, salami and mustard on a roll).

8 Community Preservation

Finish at the **Musée du Montréal Juif** (*museemontrealjuif.ca; closed Tue & Wed; $4.95*). Rotating art exhibitions celebrate Jewish culture, and events like Yiddish language classes and film screenings keep Mile End's heritage alive.

EXPERIENCES

Join the Bagel Debate BAKED GOODS

Forget hockey fights – Montréal's most enduring rivalry is soft and slightly sweet. Who makes the city's best fire-baked dough ring: Fairmount Bagel or St-Viateur Bagel? Try the baked bounty from both Mile End institutions and decide for yourself.

Begin at **Fairmount Bagel** (MAP: ❶ P103 C7; *fairmountbagel.com; 24/7*), Montréal's first bagel bakery, opened by Jewish Ukrainian immigrant Isador Shlafman in 1919 and run by his grandchildren today. Get yours with sesame or poppy seeds – or possibly *tout-garni* ('all dressed') – plus a tub of cream cheese for dipping. These bagels are best fresh; dig in immediately.

St-Viateur Bagel (MAP: ❷ P103 B6; *stviateurbagel.com*), founded in 1957 by Holocaust survivor Myer Lewkowicz, has several locations heating up gluten goodies. Their original bakery *(6am-midnight)* at 263 Rue St-Viateur Ouest, has a setup similar to Fairmount. When weather permits, take your spoils to nearby **Café Olimpico** *(cafe-olimpico-1970.myshopify.com; 6am-midnight)* and bite into your bagel on the sizable terrasse. Once you're done, the debate begins.

St-Viateur also sells bagel sandwiches at its **1127 Ave Mont-Royal** location *(7am-8pm)*.

Taste the World's Flavors Around Mile End FOOD TOUR

MAP: ❸ P103 C7

Hop across the globe on a budget-friendly cuisine crawl covering roughly 500m. For an appetizer, fly to the West Indies with Jamaican patties from **Lloydie's** *(lloydies.ca; 11:30am-9pm)* on Rue St-Viateur – bringing Caribbean flavors to Québec since the late 1980s. Next stop is **Perogie Lili** *(perogielili.com; 11am-7pm Wed-Sun)* on Ave Fairmount, a counter dishing up sweet and savory homemade Ukrainian dumplings (called *varenyky* or *perogies*). In winter, warm up with steamy borsch and a piping cup of nonalcoholic *glühwein* (mulled wine).

Continue east, past Fairmount Bagel to **Drogheria Fine** *(lasalsadellanonna.com; 11am-6pm)*, a small window where servers stuff Chinese takeout containers with pillowy Italian gnocchi doused in a sweet Calabrian red sauce. Add cheese or red-pepper flakes for extra flavor, then join the crowds eating streetside with chopsticks.

Further along is **Wilensky's Light Lunch** *(wilenskys.com; 10am-4pm Tue-Sat)*. Going strong since 1932, Wilensky's plays a role in Mordecai Richler's famous novel *The Apprenticeship of Duddy Kravitz* – scenes from the 1974 film were shot on-site. Cross the street for a return to Italy at coffee shop **Fame** *(fame.cafe; 9am-6pm)*.

The menu's star is the *zabaione* – an espresso drink made like the classic Italian dessert, frothy egg yolk on top.

Go Gallery Galavanting in Mile End
CONTEMPORARY ART

MAP: **4** P103 **D6**

Mile End's transformation from working-class enclave to creative hotbed is most evident around its eastern corner, where industrial buildings have been repurposed as free-to-visit gallery spaces.

Start at **daphne** *(daphne.art)* – Montréal's first Indigenous-run art center – promoting work by artists of First Nation, Métis and Inuit descent. It's closed Sundays. Next, head one block east to 5455 and 5445 Ave de Gaspé, a complex constructed in the 1970s and repurposed as a gallery hub. Begin at **Centre Clark** *(centreclark.com)*, an artist-run company filling two exhibition spaces with physical and virtual works; its closed Sundays and Mondays. From here, enter the complex's northern 5455 entrance and walk to the door labeled Musée Romeo's. It leads to a stairwell-gallery with 12 different street art–style murals decorating 12 floors.

Between June and September, end at **Champ des Possibles** *(Field of Possibilities; popmontreal.com/about/marche-des-possibles)*, a park at Ave de Gaspé's northern edge with seasonal events. Its defining feature: Ola Volo's 2019 mural, *Walla Volo* – a whimsical interpretation of a Mile End artist.

LIVE BANDS & ACROBATS

Casa del Popolo
MAP: **5** P103 **C8**

The 'House of the People' hosts experimental performances and indie bands (including Arcade Fire before they got big) in four intimate halls with nightly performances. In June, check out **Suoni Per Il Popolo** *(suoniperilpopolo.org)*, a music fest marching to the beat of avant-garde drummers. *(casadelpopolo.com)*

TOHU
MAP: **6** P102 **F1**

Methane from a former landfill powers this complex in St-Michel with live performances, architecture tours and a public park. Circus is the main draw – see acrobats fly around the circular performance hall, 2245m high. *(tohu.ca)*

Théâtre Rialto
MAP: **7** P103 **B5**

This 1920s beaux-arts movie theater acts as a performing arts venue promoting up-and-coming local talent. *(theatrerialto.ca)*

Give Little Italy a Big Hello
NEIGHBORHOOD TOUR

MAP: **8** P102 **C2**

Little Italy, or *Petite-Italie* (stretching between Blvd St-Laurent and Rue St-Denis from Rue St-Zotique to Rue Jean-Talon), remains Montréal's biggest bastion for Europe's brash boot, serving strong espresso, yummy pizza and the sweetest cannolis in town. Sample them all in an hour or two.

Start with espresso shots at **Caffè Italia** (*hours vary*), pulled from an Italian-made La Spaziale machine. This no-frills counter cafe, established in 1956, retains its 20th-century charm.

For southern Italian tastes, jog east to **Café San Gennaro** (*san gennaro.ca; 7:30am-7:30pm Tue-Sat, to 4pm Mon, 8am-6pm Sun; $*), serving up thick slices of Sicilian pizza and tempting *bombolones* (cream-filled doughnuts).

A few blocks northeast, save room for sweet ricotta-piped cannolis from **Alati-Caserta** (*alati caserta.com; closed Mon; $*), open since 1968.

Repent for your sweet-eating sins across the street at **Notre-Dame-de-la-Défense** (*Church of the Madonna della Difesa; diocesemontreal.org*). Look up at the temple's angelic dome, painted in the 1930s, for a controversial surprise: former Italian dictator Benito Mussolini riding a horse.

Fill Up at Marché Jean-Talon
FOOD MARKET

MAP: **9** P102 **D2**

Marché Jean-Talon (*marches publics-mtl.com*), open since 1933, is Little Italy's big belly, packed with pyramids of farm-fresh produce, meats, glazed pastries and souvenirs. In peak summer season, roughly 300 vendors ply their wares beneath four open-air hangars, and in winter the market erects walls to keep shoppers cozy. Come hungry and get ready to graze: this is Montréal's largest food market, with something for all appetites.

For a taste of quintessential Québec, start with raw-milk goats' cheese produced by **Fromagerie de la Ferme**, followed by maple syrup–coated salmon at neighboring **Délices de la Mer**. Forgo tropical sorbet at **Havre-aux-Glaces** and keep it Canadian by opting for cranberry. Try cured ham aged for six months in the **Eastern Townships at Les Cochons tout Ronds** and grab a bag of dried mushrooms scented like maple candies (called Candy Caps) at **Les Chapeaux Gourmand**. For dessert? Stop by **La Fournée des sucreries de l'érable** for nuns' farts (*'pets de soeurs,'* a Québec specialty) – each bite an angelic sugar bomb, despite the name. Visit the market's website for a map of the stalls.

LISTINGS

Best Places for...

$ Budget $$ Midrange $$$ Top End

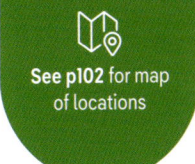

See p102 for map of locations

Eating

Mile End Brunches

Le Butterblume $$
10 C5
A yolk-yellow door opens to this bright brunch spot with an attached bakery serving sweet-savory breakfast items rotating biweekly. *lebutterblume.com, 11am-3pm Tue-Thu, 10am-4pm Sat & Sun*

Larrys $$
11 C7
Sidle up to the U-shaped bar of this hip Mile End bistro, where sun streams through St-Laurent windows onto crowds devouring breakfast sandwiches. *lawrencemtl.com, 9am-10pm Tue-Sun*

Baked Goods & Chocolates

Bernie Beigne $
12 C5
Glazed doughnuts drip in the window of this old-school sweets salon boxing up apple fritters and cinnamon ties with its funfetti doughnut assortment. *berniebeigne.shop, 10am-6pm Wed-Sun*

Cheskie's $
13 B5
Former New Yorker Cheskie Lebowitz started selling his shiny challah loaves, poppy-seed hamantaschen, babka rolls and rugelach in 2002. *+1 514-271-2253, 8am-11pm Sun-Thu, 7am-5pm Fri*

État de Choc $
14 C3
It's like the Apple store for international chocolate, each bar laid out with reverence in a minimalist space. *etatdechoc.com, 11am-5pm Sun-Wed, to 6pm Thu & Fri, 10am-5pm Sat*

Reservations Required

Vin Mon Lapin $$$
15 D3
At this classic French bistro with a modern Montréal makeover, wines are funky, veggies are fresh and plates are shareable. *vinmonlapin.com, 5-10:30pm Tue-Sat*

Montréal Plaza $$$
16 E4
Between its innovative, internationally influenced tasting menu and explosively grandiose dessert presentations, this fine diner flabbergasts. *montrealplaza.com, 5-11pm Tue-Sat*

Alma $$$
17 A4
Travel from Mexico's coast to its mountains with a multicourse tasting menu featuring heirloom corn from Tlaxcala pressed into tortillas. *almamontreal.com, 6-11pm Tue-Sat*

Pizza & Poutine

Marci $$
18 E3
Melted candle mounds light up Petite-Patrie's cool crowd, sharing pizzas and wine in this bilevel, cork-ceilinged bar-resto. *@marcisurlaplaza, 5-10:30pm Tue-Sat, to 9:30pm Sun*

Chez Claudette $$
19 D7
You might leave smelling like a fry cooker, but after trying one of its 40

poutine variations – like the smoked-meat Céline – you'll sing the praises of Montréal's best 'mess' plate. *restaurant-chez-claudette.store, 11am-11pm Tue-Sun, from 4pm Mon*

International Flavors

Pichai $$
 E4

Petite-Patrie gourmands pack into this hip restaurant for shareable plates with revelatory takes on Southeast Asian cuisine, including standout vegetarian options. *pichai.biz, 5-10:30pm Wed-Mon*

Le Super Qualité $$
21 F2

Order huge, flaky dosas, crispy *puri* (shells with yogurt filling) and more spicy South Indian street-food favorites. *lesuperqualite.com, 5-9:30pm Sun-Wed, to 10pm Thu-Sat*

Le Kahéra $
 D2

Nefirtiti's profile adorns this *dépanneur* dishing Egyptian street food. Try the *ful* – a slightly spicy pita sandwich. *@kahera mtl, 9am-7pm Mon-Fri, from 10am Sat & Sun*

Drinking

Mile End Cafes

Pastel Rita
 C5

No need to worry about finding coffee and dildos before getting that tattoo: this pastel-pink cafe has everything you need. *pastelrita.com, 8am-6pm Mon-Fri, at 9am Sat & Sun*

Café Alphabet
24 C5

Sip iced Greek-style cappuccinos, chilled milk frothed on top, while sitting on the quiet terrace where the 'Mile' ends. *ambroscoffee.com, 7am-7pm Mon-Fri, from 8am Sat & Sun*

Café Bravo
25 C8

Listen to tunes by local artists repped by Bravo Musique & Talents, located upstairs from this ground-floor cafe and record shop with 1970s aesthetics. *boutique.bravomusique.com, 8:30am-6pm*

La Petite-Patrie Cafes

Ferlucci
 D1

The 1990s are alive inside this teeny coffee shop with addictive amaretto cookies, as well as a Blockbuster-worthy VHS collection. *ferlucci.com, 7am-9pm Mon-Fri, from 8am Sat & Sun*

Zab Café
 E4

'Wake the funk up,' as a sign demands inside this local roaster's Little Italy cafe with hardcore brew sure to give you the 'coffee sweats.' *zabcafe.com, 8am-5pm*

Café des Habitudes
28 F3

Shed your shoes before entering this socks-preferred vegan coffee shop with events like open-mic nights and knitting workshops. *cafedeshabitudes.co, hours vary*

Wonderful Wine Bars

Vinvinvin
29 F4

This terrifically tiled wine den sorts sips by categories like 'mineral,' 'punk' and *'pas tranquille'* (unruly). *vinvinvin.ca, 3pm-1am Sun-Thu, to 3am Sat & Sun*

Polari
 D1

Romance is in the air at this unpretentious, all-are-welcome natural wine bar with self-branded condoms and a sign reading 'Stay queer, stay rebel.' polari.vin, 4-11pm

Mamie
31 D4

The name means 'Grandmother,' which explains this bar's perfect grannycore aesthetics, including homemade food so good you'll beg for seconds. mamiemamiemamie.com, noon-1am Thu-Sun, at 4pm Mon & Wed

Craft Beer & Cocktails

Brasserie Harricana
32 C1

Sip suds in the sophisticated dining room of this Mile-Ex brewery, hopped up since 2014. Try the smoky-umami Wild Marchen. brasserieharricana.com, hours vary

Mellön
33 E1

Enjoy frothy head on your beer? Order a Czech-style *snyt* (two parts beer, three parts foam) or *mlíko* (Czech for 'milk,' a foam-filled glass). mellonbrasserie.ca, hours vary

Brasserie Dieu du Ciel
34 C7

A fixture of Québec's craft-beer scene since 1998, this heavenly hops star shows no signs of fading. dieuduciel.com, hours vary

Bar Henrietta
35 C7

The din of diners clinking glasses bounces off white bricks in this softly lit bar bringing 'Portuguese tavern' to trendy Mile End. barhenrietta.com, 4pm-3am

Shopping

Comics, Prints & Plushies

Drawn & Quarterly
36 C5

Jump into a comic strip inside the bookshop of this cult Montréal publisher representing leading North American cartoonists. drawnandquarterly.com, 11am-6pm

Au Papier Japonais
37 C7

Lorraine Pritchard and Stan Phillips started selling handmade, conservation-quality paper imported from Japan in 1993, each piece pretty enough to frame. aupapierjaponais.com, 11am-5pm Tue-Sat

PONY
38 E3

Don't be fooled by the stuffed toys. Montréal artist Gabrielle Laïla Tittley's clothing shop is an adult Pee-wee's Playhouse, huggable phallus plushies included. ponymtl.com, noon-6pm Tue & Wed, to 7pm Thu & Fri, to 5pm Sat & Sun

Colorful Clothes & Gifts

atelier b
39 C5

On-site artisans have been crafting this smart set of sustainable, colorful clothes for adults and kids – many designs gender neutral – since 2011. atelier-b.ca, 11am-6pm Mon & Tue, to 7pm Thu & Fri, to 5pm Sat & Sun

Annex Vintage
40 C6

Surrounded by vintage shops along Blvd St-Laurent, Annex stands out with its local art, quirky magazines, feminine accessories and Y2K styles. annexvintage.com, 11am-6pm Mon-Wed, to 7pm Thu & Fri, to 5pm Sat & Sun

Ex-Voto
41 C3

Trendy fits, cutesy home decor and gifts: you're bound to fall in love with something inside this shop dedicated to local brands and sustainable makers. exvoto.ca, 11am-6pm Mon-Wed & Sat, to 7pm Thu & Fri, to 5pm Sun

Explore
Lachine Canal & Southwest Montréal

Researched by Robert Isenberg & John Garry

Sud-Ouest (Southwest) Montréal stitches together a series of suburbs mixing blue collar, bohemian and bourgeois sensibilities. The Lachine Canal – opened in 1825 to help merchant ships bypass St Lawrence River rapids – acts as its artery, now lined with parks. Cycle, stroll or paddle along the canal to pass Griffintown and Little Burgundy, once the center of Montréal's Black community, to Saint-Henri and Verdun, where a recent influx of young professionals have turned blocks of squat apartment buildings and former factories into restaurants, bars and boutiques. Westmount rises northward, with stately residential streets climbing toward the grand Oratoire St-Joseph near Parc du Mont-Royal.

Getting Around

 Métro
Take the orange line to Georges-Vanier or Lionel-Groulx for Little Burgundy; continue to Place-Sant-Henri for Saint-Henri. Take the green line to De l'Église or Verdun for Verdun. Take the blue line to Côte-des-Neiges for Oratoire St-Joseph.

 **Walk & Bicycle**
Southwest Montréal is easy to get around on foot or bike. The terrain is mostly flat, with pleasant sidewalks, well-marked bike lanes and lots of city parks. BIXI bikeshare stations are easy to find until Autoroute 15, west of Saint-Henri.

★ THE BEST

LINEAR PARK
Lachine Canal (p118)

BRUTALIST ARCHITECTURE
Habitat 67 (p120)

SPRAWLING MARKET
Marché Atwater (p120)

HISTORIC HOUSE-MUSEUM
Maison St-Gabriel (p116)

SPECTACULAR CHURCH
Oratoire St-Joseph (p120)

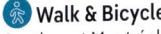
Lachine Canal (p118)
CHRISTIAN OUELLET/GETTY IMAGES

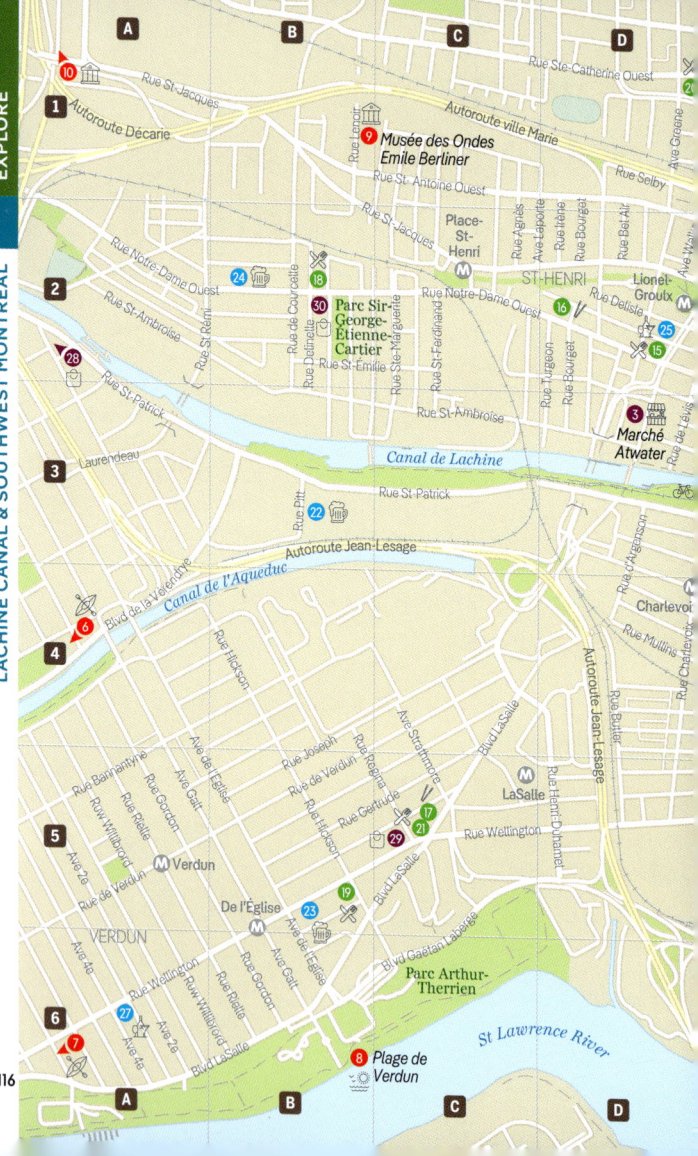

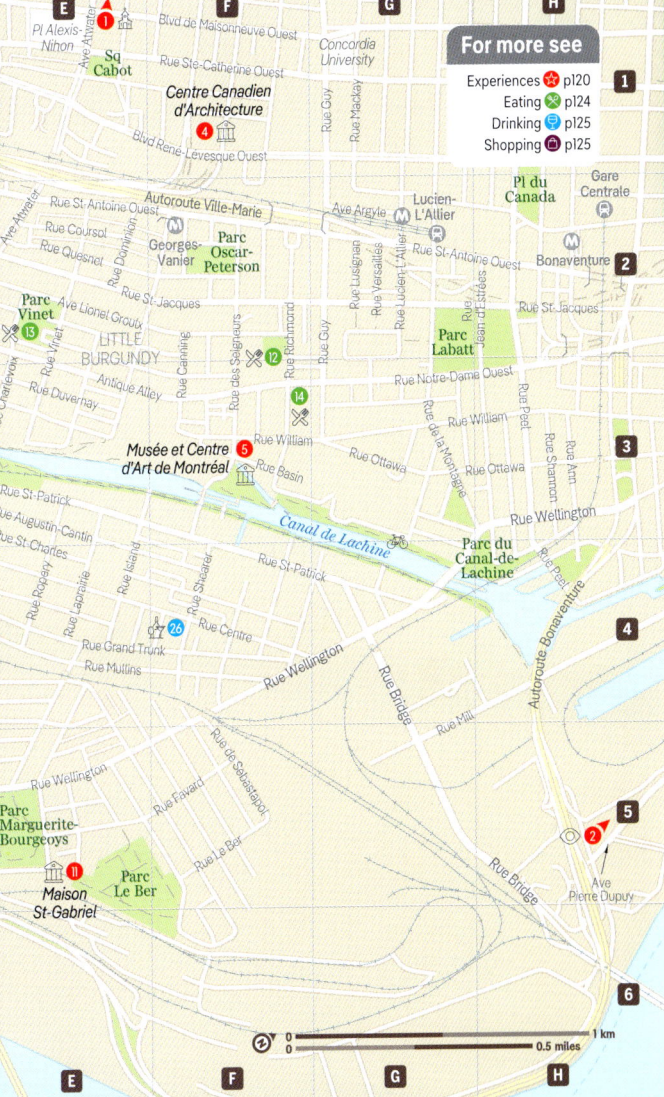

CYCLING TOUR

Cycle the Lachine Canal

This 14km canal, built in 1825 to skirt the St Lawrence's treacherous Lachine Rapids, supercharged Montréal's industrial boom – until the St Lawrence Seaway rendered it obsolete in 1959. Transformed into a linear parkway in 2002, it's now an oasis for cycling, strolling and leisurely boating.

START	END	LENGTH
Old Port	Parc René-Lévesque	30km; 3 hrs

1 Choose Your Ride

Begin by renting a bike from **Ça Roule Montréal** *(caroulemontreal.com; from $26/2hrs; book online for discounts)*, located along the Old Port. It's also possible to cycle the trail using BIXI, the city's bike-share program, though it's far less convenient if you plan to stop along the route and need a docking station, unavailable west of Autoroute 15 (7km from the Old Port).

2 Industrial Relics

Cycle past Silo No 5 – a relic of Montréal's grain port past – and under Autoroute 10, then glance south to spot the iconic **Farine Five Roses sign**. Its 15 ft-tall letters read 'Farine Five Roses Flour' from 1954 to 1977, until Bill 101 limited non-French words on signage. Brand names like 'Five Roses' were exempt, but the offending English word 'Flour' had to come down.

3 Art on the Water

Take a breather at Hangar 1825 to appreciate how creatives have reimagined the canal. The building is wrapped in a mural by French artist Ankhone, *Alchemy of Time* (2020), honoring the site's industrial past and celebrating its green reinvention. With time to spare, step inside nearby **Arsenal Art Contemporain** *(arsenalcontemporary.com; $15/10 adult/child)*, a 19th-century shipyard transformed into a sprawling visual arts hub.

4 Food for Fuel

Stop by **Marché Atwater** to assemble a picnic for later in the journey, then cross the Atwater footbridge to recharge with a coffee on the outdoor terrace of **Café Ma Bicyclette** *(8am-8pm)*. If you want to see the canal from a boater's point of view, this is where to do it: next door, H2O Adventures offers kayak and paddleboat rentals *(aventuresh2o.ca; from $20/30min)*.

5 Into the Past

Pedal along the green-flanked waterway for roughly 9.5km, passing a series of shimmering bridges en route to **Musée de Lachine** *(ville.montreal.qc.ca; free)*. Set on the banks of the St Lawrence, this history museum occupies the French Colonial Maison Le Ber-Le Moyne – one of the region's oldest houses, built between 1669 and 1671 as a fur trading post.

6 Sculptures & Sunset

Continue through nearby **Parc René-Lévesque**, a skinny peninsula jutting into Lac St-Louis (where the St Lawrence River broadens), spectacular at sunset. Mammoth-sized modernist sculptures decorate the park, along with tables perfect for picnicking. To finish the trip, coast back along the canal to Old Montréal's cobblestone streets.

EXPERIENCES

Join Pilgrims Climbing to Oratoire St-Joseph
BASILICA

MAP: ❶ P117 E1

Canada's tallest **church** (saint-joseph.org) soars nearly 130m into the heavens alongside the city's landmark mountain. This Catholic basilica is the world's largest shrine honoring Jesus' earthly father and a major site for pilgrims, some of whom crawl up the church's 300 steps on their knees.

This granite temple's story starts in 1904, when Alfred Bessette – aka Brother André (1845–1937) – established a small wooden chapel across from Collège Notre-Dame. Brother André was said to have miraculous healing powers, and as word spread, the chapel quickly became overwhelmed by visitors. Construction on the current Italian Renaissance–inspired basilica began in 1924 and was finally completed in 1966.

The oratory spreads across eight floors linked by elevators, escalators and staircases. If you're short on time, zip to Level 4's **Votive Chapel**, warmed by hundreds of candles leading to Brother André's black-granite tomb. After paying your respects, head to Level 8 to marvel at the basilica interior's stark art deco design. There's also a Level 3 cafeteria, a Level 5 terrace and a Level 6 **museum**.

Behold Brutalism at Habitat 67
MODERN ARCHITECTURE

MAP: ❷ P117 H5

Habitat 67 may be the city's most provocative modern structure – a LEGO-like arrangement of prefabricated blocks on Cité du Havre, a St Lawrence River peninsula looking toward Old Montréal and visible from the Old Port's **Grand Quai** (p41). Fans admire its imaginative, angular design – an enduring monument to **Expo 67** (p53), for which it was built. Love it or loathe it, Habitat remains a coveted piece of real estate: in 2023, one apartment garnered attention for its $1.4 million asking price.

Israel-born architect Moshe Safdie designed the Brutalist concrete structure for his college thesis, combining box-like suburban homes with the stackability of high-rises – his utopian dream for a densely-populated urban future.

Habitat hosts regular **90-minute tours** *(habitat67.com; $58; reserve in advance)* from May to November in French and English. Guides lead visitors through outdoor spaces as well as the inside of one residence. Reach Cité du Havre via the 777 bus or bike path linked to the Lachine Canal route.

Shop Through the Ages at Marché Atwater
FOOD MARKET

MAP: ❸ P116 D3

Marché Atwater *(marches publics-mtl.com)* has been the

commercial keystone of Southwest Montréal since 1933, drawing hungry hordes to food stalls within its long brick building, topped by a 45m-high clock tower overlooking Little Burgundy.

Part of its appeal is the century-old aesthetic: Québec architect Ludger Lemieux designed the hangar-sized structure in a distinctive art deco style, with sharp vertical lines and bold rectangular windows. Greengrocers occupy the contained outer hall in winter, with stalls and a food court extending into the parking lot in warmer months. Deeper in, specialty shops sell quality meats, cheeses and jarred goods. For sit-down meals, savor an espresso and pastry from **Brûlerie aux Quatre Vents** (Four Winds Roastery; *brulerie4vents.com; $*) or choose between a grilled sandwich and maple sugar tartlet at **Boulangerie Première Moisson** (First Harvest Bakery; *premieremoisson.com; $*).

Atwater is conveniently located at the edge of Little Burgundy and a stone's throw from the Lachine Canal – ideal for a pitstop while cycling the canal's greenway.

Appreciate Design at the Centre Canadien d'Architecture ARCHITECTURE MUSEUM

MAP: 4 P117 F1

Buildings get framed like fine art at the **Centre Canadien d'Architecture** *(CCA; cca.qc.ca; $10; free Thu 5pm-9pm & first Sun of month)* – a museum and research space near Downtown's western edge. Exhibits explore everything from individual construction projects to provocative looks at climate change. Free audio guides are available upon request. It's closed Mondays and Tuesdays.

It's all displayed in a jaw-dropping complex anchored by the Shaughnessy House – a Second Empire–style mansion from 1876 and a reminder of the elegant homes that once lined Blvd René-Lévesque. In the 1970s, Montréal architect Phyllis Lambert purchased the estate to prevent its demolition. She then spearheaded the CCA,

---

 MUSÉE ET CENTRE D'ART DE MONTRÉAL

Wander through rooms fit for a Wes Anderson flick on a self-guided tour of Griffintown's **Musée et Centre d'art de Montréal** (MAP: 5 P117 F3; *Montréal Art Center & Museum; montrealartcenter.com; $9.20*) – a community hub for artists of all media and skill levels. The facility is housed in a renovated historic building from 1879, with rooms divided into studios, a theater for live performances and exhibition galleries showcasing everything from 19th-century art to modern works, including paper sketches by Picasso and Monet. Feeling inspired? Join local creatives at a live drawing or plein air painting class, often offered on Saturdays *($15; BYO art supplies)*.

PADDLE THE ST LAWRENCE RIVER
Rafting Montréal
MAP: ❻ P116 A4

Join a guided whitewater rafting excursion around the Lachine Rapids between May and October. Minimum age is six *(raftingmontreal.com; adults/teens/kids $61/51/44)*.

Espace Navi
MAP: ❼ P116 A6

Set off from Verdun's shores on a solo kayak journey or join a guided tour, particularly magical on summer nights when fireworks erupt from **La Ronde** (p52; *espacenavi.ca; 1/2hr $28/42)*.

integrating the mansion into the museum's contemporary design.

After touring the museum, cross Blvd René-Lévesque to see the free-to-visit **CCA Garden** on Ernest-Cormier Esplanade. At the top of the park, architectural models – including a nod to Montréal's grain silos – sit atop pedestals overlooking the industrial Saint-Henri neighborhood.

Stroll and Sun Around Verdun NEIGHBORHOOD TOUR
MAP: ❽ P116 B6

The riverside borough of Verdun has been burning hot in recent years – most apparent along **Rue Wellington**, where a slew of trendy pubs and restaurants have transformed the working-class district of 70,000 residents into a coveted place to live. The strip is splendid in summer, when it shuts down to traffic and pedestrians take over. To make the most of a seasonal sojourn to the area, cool off after Wellington promenade at **Plage de Verdun** (Verdun Beach) – a sandy crescent along the St Lawrence.

The beach is modest, with a capacity of about 400 people, and the water is calm and shallow – perfect for wading on scorching days. If you don't care for river swimming, there's a public pool a short skip away, part of the surrounding Parc Arthur-Thierren, a manicured green space.

All Ears at the Musée des Ondes Emile Berliner AUDIO MUSEUM
MAP: ❾ P116 B1

Don't touch that dial: everywhere you look in Saint-Henri's **Musée des Ondes Emile Berliner** *(Wave Museum, MOEB; moeb.ca; $15)* are shelves of vintage radios, restored turntables and vinyl records spanning the past century. Founded in 1992 by a group of hobbyists known as the Club des Vieilles Lampes (Old Lamp Club), the museum is named for Emile Berliner (1851–1929) – the German-American innovator who invented the gramophone record. Every corner honors audio tech in all its forms, from household stereos to radio transmissions with astronauts, with knowledgeable docents on hand to explain every button and antenna.

The museum's symbolic setting is the old RCA Building. In its heyday, RCA Victor maintained an important branch in Montréal, where vinyl records were recorded and mixed. It's only open Wednesday to Friday and advance reservations are recommended.

Pay Your Respects at the Musée de L'Holocauste   JEWISH HISTORY

MAP: 10 P116 A1

In the great constellation of the Jewish diaspora, Montréal is a bright star. Jewish immigrants arrived from Great Britain as early as the 18th century, and the city is now home to a robust community of descendents (p106). But as the **Musée de l'Holocauste** (*musee holocauste; adult/student $12/10*) notes in its chilling permanent exhibition, Canada joined the US in rejecting Jewish refugees in the 1930s, condemning untold numbers to Nazi death camps.

Using an exhaustive collection of period artifacts, exhibits chronicle the rise of fascism in Europe and the disintegration of Jewish life. This is Canada's only museum dedicated to the Holocaust, and the photographs, pamphlets and newspaper clippings don't pull any punches.

Currently housed in a nondescript office building across from Mackenzie King Park (and closed Saturdays) there are plans to move to a new building on Blvd St-Laurent in the Plateau in 2027 – an area where Jewish life flourished in the 20th century.

Time Travel at Maison St-Gabriel   COLONIAL HISTORY

MAP: 11 P117 E5

Life around Montréal wasn't easy for colonists in the late 17th century. It can be hard to even fathom what the average French person experienced during those early years, though a visit to the **Maison St-Gabriel** (*maisonsaintgabriel. ca; adult/child 6-17yr $15/5*) paints a clearer picture with costumed interpreters bringing their daily routines to life.

Maison St-Gabriel, one of Canada's oldest surviving farmsteads, was established by devout Catholic Frenchwoman Marguerite Bourgeoys (1620–1700), who founded the Congregation de Notre Dame – North America's first uncloistered religious community for women. The many pioneers who passed through these doors include the Filles du Roi (King's Daughters) – unmarried women who moved to New France to populate the colony.

Each floor of the museum feels like a time machine, lovingly preserved with period furniture and historical objects. Reserve tours online in English or French. It's closed on Mondays and Tuesdays.

LISTINGS

Best Places for...

💲 Budget 💲💲 Midrange 💲💲💲 Top End

See p116 for map of locations

Eating

Critically Acclaimed Restaurants

Candide 💲💲💲
🟢 12 F2
Praise regional flavors inside this church presbytery transformed into a farm-to-fork fine diner with a warm red-brick interior and seasonal terrace. *restaurantcandide.com, 6-10pm Tue-Sat*

Joe Beef 💲💲💲
🟢 13 E2
This beloved restaurant started churning out decadent Québécois dishes in 2005 and continues to dazzle. Extra hungry? Try the steak *au poivre*. *joebeef.com, 5-10:30pm Tue-Sat*

Foxy 💲💲💲
🟢 14 F3
Foodies burn hot for wood-fired fare ranging from ingenious veggie dishes to meats and sweets made with ingredients sourced from local farms. *foxy.restaurant, 5:30-11pm*

Foiegwa 💲💲💲
🟢 15 D2
Enjoy brunch, seafood and cocktails at this vintage Americanized French diner with framed caricatures of famous Montréalers. *foiegwa.com, 5:30-11pm Mon-Thu, 10am-2pm & 5:30-11pm Fri, 9:30am-3pm & 6-11pm Sat & Sun*

Asian Cuisine

Satay Brothers 💲
🟢 16 D2
Head to the Rue Notre-Dame sit-down spot of this legendary Montréal mini chain serving Singaporean street food. The flavorful menu and reasonable prices appeal to foodies on a budget. *sataybrothers.com, 11am-11pm Thu-Sun, 5-11pm Mon-Wed*

Les Street Monkeys 💲💲
🟢 17 C5
Elaborate bowls and shareable plates interweave Cambodian, Thai and Montréaler influences on Verdun's uber-cool Rue Wellington. *streetmonkeys.ca, 5:30-11pm Thu-Sat, 5:30-10pm Sun, Mon & Wed*

Brunch & Lunch Fare

Arthurs 💲💲
🟢 18 B2
Arrive early on weekends to beat Saint-Henri's brunch crowds, scrambling here for Jewish luncheonette staples with international zest in diner-style surrounds. *arthursmtl.com, 9am-3pm Mon-Fri, to 4pm Sat & Sun*

Janine Café 💲💲
🟢 19 B5
This queen of the Verdun brunch scene has high-backed chairs, like a proper British tea parlor, from which diners devour gorgeous platters gleaming with golden yolks. *janinecafe.ca, 9am-3pm*

Glorious Gluten

Marché Bagels on Greene 💲
🟢 20 D1
Come here for bagels, plus coffees, torpedo-roll sandwiches and a rainbow of pasta

salads. *bagelsongreene.com, 7am-5pm Mon-Sat, 8am-4pm Sun*

Rita $

21 C5

The only thing that rivals the pizzas at this trendy Italian place – named for the same-named grandmothers of its co-owners – is the decadent, maple-infused *pouding chômeur* (poor man's pudding). *ritarestaurant.ca, 5-10pm Mon-Sat*

Drinking

Breweries & Dive Bars

Messorem

22 B3

Funky sours and hoppy IPAs flow from taps at this industrial, graffiti-splashed Sud-Ouest microbrewery with a spacious terrace near the Lachine Canal. *messorem.co, noon-midnight*

BENELUX Brasserie Artisanale

23 B5

Don't be fooled by the stuffy vintage bank facade on Rue Wellington. This lowkey brewpub is all about heady IPAs and down-home hot dogs. *brasseriebenelux.com/wellington,* 3pm-3am Mon-Thu, noon-3am Fri-Sun

Bon Délire

24 B2

Translated as 'good crazy,' this is a cavernous dive bar where you can aim for the cue ball on a leopard-print pool table while savoring the superlative beer selection. *bondelirebar.com, 5pm-3am*

Craft Cocktails & Natural Wine

Atwater Cocktail Club

25 D2

Walk toward the red light at the end of a graffiti'd alley to enter this sexy cocktail temple with mirrored ceilings. *atwatercocktailclub.com, 5pm-3am*

Milky Way Cocktail Bar

26 F4

Prepare for lift off at this second-floor cocktail club with a skylight looking toward the stars. Order pizza from Trattoria Fugazzi, made next door. *milkywaycocktails.com, 5:30pm-3am*

Verdun Beach Wine Bar

27 A6

Drop into this Parisian-style bar on Rue Wellington to sip natural wines accompanied by small plates, or sign up for a wine-tasting workshop online. *barverdunbeach.com, hours vary*

Shopping

Artisanal Candy & Clothes

Candylabs

28 A2

Watch candymakers craft hard sweets, each pretty as a piece of jewelry, or drop in on weekends for a 75-minute lollipop-making class. *candylabs.ca, Tue-Sun 11am-6pm*

Harricana

29 C5

Find a Montréal-made hat for any season – berets, beanies, felt caps and fedoras – along with more clothing upcycled from furs, silks and tweeds. *harricana.qc.ca, 10am-6pm Mon-Fri, to 5pm Sat & Sun*

GanK

30 B2

Local designers provide the street-smart, on-trend fashions lining racks inside this tiny Saint-Henri boutique with masc and femme fits. *gank.shop, 10am-5pm Mon-Wed, to 6pm Thu & Fri, to 4pm Sat & Sun*

Explore
Québec City

Researched by Pamela MacNaughtan & Robert Isenberg

Skip the trans-atlantic flight and land in francophone Québec City, North America's version of storybook Europe, where four centuries of Indigenous, French and British influences ricochet off stone ramparts and cobbled streets. Cap Diamant, a cliff above the St Lawrence River, divides historic Old Québec in two. The fortified city crowns the cliff (Haute-Ville); the oldest neighborhoods, Petit-Champlain and Place-Royale, sit at its base (Basse-Ville), where Samuel de Champlain established a French foothold in 1608. Beyond Old Québec, St-Jean-Baptiste, St-Roch and Limoilou are vibrant neighborhoods with a contemporary edge. Outside the city, river islands and a First Nations community appear plucked from pastoral fables.

Getting Around

Bus
An extensive network zips between popular sights and local neighborhoods. Download the RTC Nomade app for real-time information and RTC Paiement to buy digital tickets.

Bicycle
In summer, bike-share program àVelo has hundreds of e-bikes for rent throughout the city, with handy stations near Parc Montmorency, Château Frontenac and Musée de la Civilisation. Download the àVélo app for info.

Walk
Most sights are within walking distance. Avoid the frustration of driving a car and hunting for parking.

★

THE BEST

ROMANTIC ARCHITECTURE
Château Frontenac (p135)

OLD-WORLD RAMPARTS
Fortifications of Québec (p130)

IMMERSIVE MUSEUM
Musée de la Civilisation (p130)

COBBLESTONE STREETS
Quartier Petit-Champlain (p134)

WINTER FESTIVAL
Carnaval de Québec (p138)

Château Frontenac (p135)
YWEI61/SHUTTERSTOCK

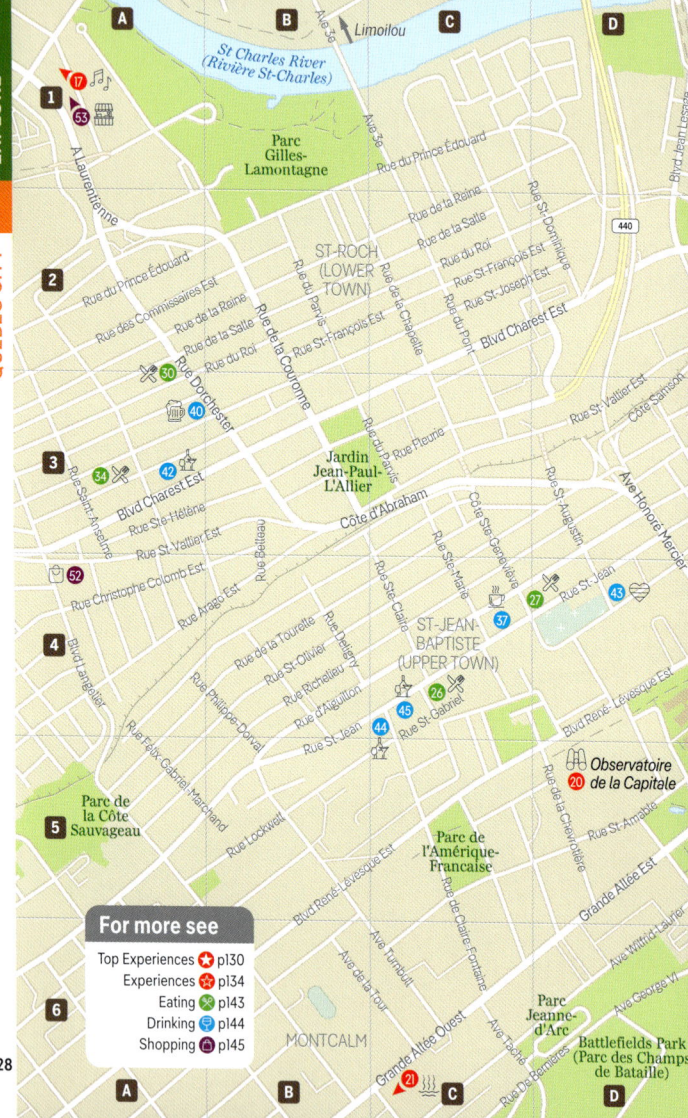

★ **TOP EXPERIENCE**

Fortifications of Québec

The 4.6km ramparts encircling Old Québec recall the military grit of colonial eras. Walk the elaborate defense system, constructed over multiple stages between the 17th and 19th centuries, to journey back in time while enjoying city views.

MAP P128 **E3**

PLANNING TIP
Join a guided English-speaking tour of the fortifications from mid-May to mid-October *(adult/child $21/12; check the website for times)*. To walk the entire circuit, go counter-clockwise from Terrasse Dufferin.

Securing Québec

At the height of the fur trade, Québec City (capital of New France) was under constant threat of British attack. Cap Diamant and its cliffs formed a natural shield, but the northern side of the city remained exposed. Beginning in the 1690s, the French built stone ramparts to protect the settlement, but they weren't enough. In 1759, British General James Wolfe's troops scaled a narrow path at Cap Diamant, reached the plateau, and defeated the French on the **Plaines d'Abraham** (p134) outside the city walls.

After securing control in 1763, the British went to work reinforcing the city's defenses. By the 1870s, calls for urban modernization threatened to demolish the ramparts, but Governor General Lord Dufferin led a successful campaign to preserve and embellish what's now Old Québec's defining feature.

Exploring the Ramparts

If you only have time for the highlights, start in the **Château St-Louis** ruins beneath **Terrasse Dufferin**, where interactive displays offer a glimpse back in time. From here, walk along Rue St-Louis to the wall, then follow it to **Artillery Park** and end at the **Dauphine Redoubt** (1712) – a former barracks and one of North America's oldest military buildings.

Scan the QR code for opening hours and park updates.

★ TOP EXPERIENCE

Musée de la Civilisation

Investigate the human experience at this world-class museum suitable for all ages, where past exhibits have covered everything from poop to Tintin. Permanent installations are devoted to Indigenous voices and Québécois history. Budget for a few hours.

MAP P128 **H2**

Appreciate the Architecture

Designed in the 1980s by Israeli-Canadian architect Moshe Safdie, the visionary behind Montréal's **Habitat 67** (p120), the museum incorporates historic buildings and contemporary additions. The exterior walls are clad in local gray limestone, blending in with the surrounding neighborhood, while copper roofing mirrors Château Frontenac. The foyer incorporates the restored stone wall of Maison Estèbe (built here in 1751) and showcases a French Regime boat – one of many artifacts uncovered during on-site archaeological digs.

Permament Exhibitions

In Other Words, Québec is the museum's largest display, spread across six pavilions showcasing the province's evolution through human interactions. It begins with the first contact between European colonizers and First Nations people in the 16th century, then explores Québec life as it relates to seasons, economics, protests and communities.

For a poignant foray into Indigenous culture, wander through **This Is Our Story** – a permanent exhibit created in collaboration with 11 First Nations, recounting histories and offering first-hand perspectives through art, artifacts and sound clips.

PLANNING TIPS
Purchase tickets ahead of time to save $3. Use the museum's mobile app *(mon.mcq.org)* to access exhibit-related content, including a site map.

Scan the QR code for opening hours and to purchase tickets.

Stroll Through Old Québec

In Old Québec 19th-century structures have been lovingly restored, contemporary art decorates colonial facades and 17th-century streets lead to chic cafes and boutiques. Wander past fountains, fortifications and frescoes, pausing for snacks and sweeping river views. It makes for a romantic sunset stroll.

START	END	LENGTH
Fontaine de Tourny	Batterie Royale	2km; 1 hr

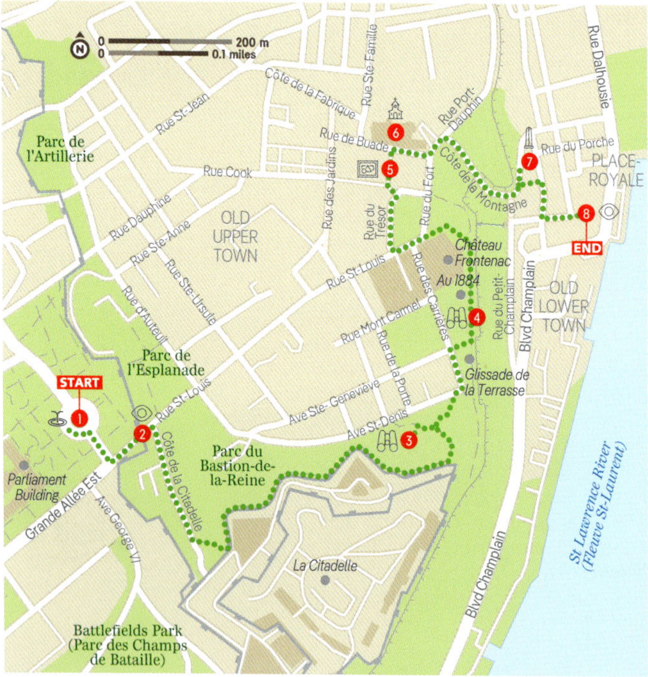

1 Fabulous Fountain
Begin at the **Fontaine de Tourny**, a cast-iron fountain that made waves at the Paris World Fair in 1855. Statues of historical figures watch over the 7m-tall waterwork's 43 jets from the nearby Parliament Building.

2 Grand Entrance
Cross beneath **Porte St-Louis**, an impressive gate connected to the city's fortified walls. First erected in 1693, it was reconstructed in 1878 with a tower and turret, enhancing its grandeur. A staircase leads to a walkway atop the fortifications, offering a bird's-eye view of Rue St-Louis.

3 Spectacular Sights
Make a right on Côte de la Citadelle to Parc du Bastion-de-la-Reine then follow the walking path toward **Terrasse Pierre-Dugua-de-Mons**, with a panorama showcasing Château Frontenac), the Citadelle and the St Lawrence River.

4 Pedestrian Promenade
A wooden staircase leads to more views from **Terrasse Dufferin** – a 425m-long boardwalk perched high above the St Lawrence. In winter, adrenaline junkies speed down a wooden toboggan run and, in summer, street performers serenade passersby. No matter the season, stop by Au 1884 for a sweet treat – perhaps a *chocolat chaud* (hot chocolate) or some chocolate-dipped ice cream.

5 Alfresco Paintings
Skip to **Rue du Trésor**, where artists started exhibiting work in the 1960s. Today, the narrow alley is like an open-air gallery, most vibrant from mid-May to mid-October and on holiday weekends.

6 Faith Revived
The end of Rue du Trésor leads to the **Basilique-Cathédrale Notre-Dame-de-Québec** (p137). Step inside to ogle the gilded interior, restored to its original splendor after a 1922 fire.

7 Art For All
Continue onward to Rue Notre-Dame to see the **Fresque des Québécois** – a 420-sq-m trompe-l'oeil featuring famous figures in Québec history, including explorer Jacques Cartier. Look up while wandering along the street to search for tiny human figures hidden in nooks by artist Isaac Cordal, created in 2025 for public art non-profit EXMURO.

8 Riverfront Defense
End along the riverfront at **Batterie Royale**, initially built in 1691 and restored in 1977, where cannon reproductions and informational panels recall when French soldiers surveyed the waterfront for British ships. These days, you can watch ferries chugging peacefully across the river to Lévis.

EXPERIENCES

Wander the Historic Plaines d'Abraham PARK AND MUSEUM

Whether picnicking under a leafy elm or joining the city's throngs for a festival, it might be hard to imagine the **Plaines d'Abraham** (MAP: ❶ P129 E6; part of Battlefields Park) as an 18th-century battleground. But in September 1759, British General James Wolfe stunned French General Louis-Joseph Montcalm with a surprise cliffside assault, leading to a 20-minute clash that left both men mortally wounded and New France under British control. The Treaty of Paris in 1763 sealed the deal, redrawing the map of power in North America. Today the clifftop park draws visitors with its panoramic overlooks and peaceful paths, used for strolling and cross-country skiing.

Learn more about the deadly battle at the **Musée des Plaines d'Abraham** (MAP: ❷ P129 E5; *plaines dabraham.ca; $17 Jul & Aug, $13.75 Sep-Jun*), which chronicles the events with period clothing and immersive videos spread across three floors. To cover the grounds quickly, hop on a 45-minute **guided bus tour** *(adult/child $12.75/free)*, looping from the museum to views from Cap Diamant, past 19th-century Martello towers and along the grounds where war once raged.

Shop Around Le Petit-Champlain and Place-Royale STORIED STREETS

Travel back to 18th-century Québec on a 20-minute stroll, imagining when the narrow cobblestone streets of **Petit-Champlain** (MAP: ❸ P129 G4) and **Place-Royale** became a thriving commercial sector. Start at Place-Royale, with its gable-roofed stone houses, and take note of the ceramic plaques affixed beside doorways, listing their dates of origin. The settlement of 'Kebec' started in the spot now occupied by the Église Notre-Dame-des-Victoires (originally built from 1688 to 1723), dominating the square. After the battle of 1759 against the British, the neighborhood surrounding the church became a busy wharf and warehouse district, with workers living in tenement houses on Rue du Petit-Champlain.

On Petit-Champlain, climb to the top of **Escalier Casse-Cou** (MAP: ❹ P129 G3; Breakneck Steps, built in 1635), for a streetscape view from the oldest stairs in Québec City. Descend the staircase to wander past restaurants, pubs and shops selling sundries from historically restored homes blending French and English architectural styles. End at the Fresque du Petit-Champlain (2001) – a large mural depicting the neighborhood's working-class history.

Float Along the St Lawrence
RIVER CRUISE

MAP: **5** P129 **H3**

From May to October, set sail on the St Lawrence with **Croisières AML** (*croisieresaml.com*) to admire the cityscape.

On the 90-minute **Québec City Guided Sightseeing River Cruise** *($50)*, guests enjoy panoramic views of Montmorency Falls and Île d'Orléans while listening to commentary on the area's maritime and colonial history. Audioguides are also available in eight languages.

There's also an evening **DJ and Cocktail cruise** *($50)*, complete with an outdoor dance floor, plus boat rides for **dinner** *(from $130)* and **weekend brunch** *($80)*. In August, try the 3-course **Dinner and Fireworks cruise**, which departs on evenings when Grands Feux Loto-Québec (*lesgrandsfeux.com*) shoots kaleidoscopic flares above the city. Check Croisières AML's website for a full lineup of offerings.

For a faster, cheaper alternative, take a scenic 15-minute ride on the **Québec–Lévis ferry** (*traversiers.com; adult/child $4.15/$2.90*). Boats depart from Gare Fluviale de Québec terminal every 30 to 60 minutes.

Snap a Photo of the Château Frontenac
HISTORIC HOTEL

MAP: **6** P129 **G3**

Towering atop Cap Diamant like a lord surveying his land, **Château Frontenac** (*fairmont.com/frontenac-quebec*) is so spectacular it supports the claim of being the most photographed hotel in the world. Built in 1893 by the Canadian Pacific Railway to lure elite travelers, it later passed to Fairmont and now operates under the Accor portfolio, continuing to draw sightseers with its imposing central tower and turrets. Things get even more grand inside, with brushed gold accents, grand staircases and crystal chandeliers galore. A 70-minute guided excursion with **Cicerone Tours**

 QUÉBEC CITY'S ORIGINS

In 1608, explorer Samuel de Champlain founded France's first permanent settlement in North America along the St Lawrence River. He called it Québec – from the Indigenous Algonquian word 'Kebec,' meaning 'where the river narrows' – now considered the cradle of French Canada. Champlain's bottom line was big business. Furs were wildly lucrative, so he established a fortified trading post at present-day Place-Royale, tapping into Indigenous trade routes to acquire items like beaver pelts. These coveted skins became New France's financial engine – transforming North America's landscape and economy while stoking decades of shifting alliances, cultural upheaval and violence for First Nations communities.

(cicerone.ca; adult/youth/child; $22/11/free) reveals a history of famous guests and important meetings, most notably the Québec Conferences of WWII, when William Lyon Mackenzie King, prime minister of Canada, hosted Winston Churchill and Franklin D Roosevelt.

Even if you're not staying here (nightly rates range from $600 to $4500), you can still explore the public spaces, sip cocktails at 1608 Wine Bar, or dine at Restaurant Champlain or Bistro Le Sam.

Tour the Assemblée Nationale
PARLIAMENT BUILDING

MAP: P129 E4

Take a free 60-minute guided tour of the **Assemblée nationale du Québec** *(assnat.qc.ca/en/index.html, reservations required)* home of Québec's provincial legislature, to see the interior of the Second Empire structure (completed in 1886) and learn more about the province's parliamentary past. Talks detail the 1995 referendum, when the Parti Québécois wanted Québec to secede from Canada, and important political leaders such as René Lévesque (founder of the Parti Québécois) and Jean Lesage (dubbed the father of the Quiet Revolution). Tours are offered in French and English. Self-guided tours are available by reservation. Bring photo ID.

Even if you don't step inside, you can admire the building's exterior, which is adorned with 26 bronze statues depicting historical figures – including city founder Samuel de Champlain. Look above the main entrance and below the coat of arms to see the province's motto: *Je me souviens* ('I remember'), evoking memories of French heritage, British conquest and the many other subsequent events that shaped Québec.

LANGUAGE REVOLUTION

After Britain seized control of Québec in 1763, English became the language of power and French became second-class. By the 1960s, francophone frustrations reached a boiling point, one of many sparks igniting the Révolution Tranquille (Quiet Revolution) helmed by Parti Libéral du Québec leader Jean Lesage. Citizens demanded secularism, education reform and greater economic control. Catholic influence waned. Political action surged. French, long marginalized, was elevated in public life. Québécois nationalism gained momentum, culminating in 1976 when René Lévesque's Parti Québécois won control of the provincial government. In 1977, Bill 101 made French the province's official language, reshaping Québec's identity.

Soak up Hospitality at Le Monastère des Augustines

MUSEUM AND HOTEL

MAP: **8** P129 **E2**

Wellness has been central to the mission at **Le Monastère des Augustines** *(monastere.ca; adult/child $17/free)* for over three centuries. It started with the arrival of three Augustinian Sisters in 1639, who established New France's first hospital here in 1644. The tradition got a glow up in 2015, when the cloistered convent was reimagined as a museum-and-therapy hotel, open to all. Decompress from life's stressors while paying homage to Québec's pioneering caregivers.

Start at the **museum** *(closed Mon)* tracing 320 years of healthcare with hundreds of artifacts and the moving exhibit **Healing Body and Soul**, exploring the nuns' way of life until Québec's health system absorbed the hospital in 1962.

Guests can also take yoga and meditation classes, book a massage or dine on wholesome fare at **Le Vivoir** *(11am-10pm; $$)*. Turn the 17th-century halls into an overnight sanctuary by booking a stay in a modernized nun's cell *(starting around $150)*.

Visit the First Catholic Parish North of Mexico

CHURCH

MAP: **9** P129 **G3**

You don't need to be a devout Catholic to appreciate the **Basilique-Cathédrale Notre-Dame-de-Québec** *(notre-dame-de-quebec.org/home; free)*, with its domed tower, baldachin-capped altar, vibrant stained glass and Holy Door (inaugurated in 2013; set to reopen in 2049). French explorer Samuel de Champlain built a chapel here in 1633, replaced by a stone Jesuit church in 1647. When St François de Laval, who was canonized in 2014, was appointed head of the Diocese of Québec in 1674, it was elevated to cathedral status, then named a minor basilica in 1874. The neoclassical design – crafted by three generations of Baillairgé family carpenters (1759–1843) – was gutted in 1922 by an American arsonist allegedly tied to the Ku Klux Klan, then painstakingly rebuilt from photographs. Don't miss the funerary chapel, housing Laval's tomb, or the crypt *(Wed-Sun 1:30–3:30pm)*, resting place of four New France governors.

Embrace Winter's Chill

OUTDOOR RECREATION

Québec City winters might be cold, but that's no reason to cower indoors. Live like a local by giving the frosted months a hearty bear hug. Start by dressing appropriately – thermal underwear, heavy coat, sturdy boots and all. Once you've properly suited up, choose your adventure.

The outdoor skating rink at **Place d'Youville** (MAP: **10** P129 **E3**;

free, skate rentals around $8) is a picturesque spot to savor the season from mid-November to mid-March; the rink looks toward the city's ramparts. At **Plaines d'Abraham** (p134), rent cross-country skis *(plainsof abraham.ca; from adult/child $24/14 for 2hrs)* or snowshoes *(adult/child $12/8 for 2hrs)* to leisurely explore the landscape. On **Terrasse Dufferin** (p130), thrill-seekers can barrel down the **Glissade de la Terrasse** (MAP: ⑪ P129 G4; *au1884.ca; from $3.50*) – a wooden slide, first installed in 1884, where riders hop on a toboggan to reach speeds of up to 70km/hr. Warm up post ride with hot chocolate from the nearby **Au 1884** cafe (MAP: ⑫ P129 G4; *10am-6pm Sun-Thu, to 9pm Fri & Sat)*.

Join Canada's Oldest Winter Festival

CELEBRATION

MAP: ⑬ P129 E4

The **Carnaval de Québec** *(carna val.qc.ca)* is a bright light during winter's darkest months, celebrating all things frosty for 10 days. The festival dates back to 1894 and has since snowballed into an annual extravaganza where people take snow baths in swimsuits, cheer for canoe races on the icy St Lawrence River and join night parades with live performances. Ice sculptures decorate Old Québec, restaurants build ice bars and locals lug around plastic canes filled with Caribou – a Québécois winter tipple made with fortified wine and whiskey. The party is overseen by carnival king Bonhomme – a snowman wearing a red knitted toque and *ceinture fléchée* (French arrow sash) around his waist. Purchase a plastic carnival effigie *($39 in 2025)* – in the shape of Bonhomme – which acts as a passport for festival activities.

Dig the chill factor? Book a room at **Hôtel de Glace** *(valcartier.com /fr; starting at $479; open Jan– mid-Mar)* the oldest ice hotel in North America, located 20 minutes from Old Québec. A warm room next door at Village Vacances Valcartier is included in the rate.

Cycle Québec City

BIKE ROUTES

MAP: ⑭ P129 H4

Bid Old Québec adieu by cycling off to distant neighborhoods. Electric bikeshare program **àVélo** *(aveloquebec.ca; from 33¢/min)* is perfect for traveling short distances. For longer excursions, consider renting a set of wheels from **Echo Sports Tours** *(echo sportstours.ca; from $17/hr)*.

Promenade Samuel-de-Champlain is a popular path, stretching 6.8km along the St Lawrence between Côte Gilmour and Pont Pierre-Laporte. The route passes public art installations and **Station de la Plage**: a beach and infinity pool overlooking the river. (If using àVélo, the nearest docking station to the beach is a short walk east). Budget for an hour or two.

For a slightly longer haul, follow part of the 50km **Corridor du Littoral** (which also includes the Promenade Samuel-de-Champlain) northeast from the Old Port to the entrance of **Parc de la Chute-Montmorency** (p148). This section covers 13km one way; budget for at least three hours. Cycling here requires a bike rental. The Corridor du Littoral is part of the **Route Verte** *(routeverte.com)*, a 5400km network of cycling trails weaving through Québec.

Tour La Citadelle — MILITARY MUSEUM
MAP: 15 P129 F5

Sometimes called the Gibraltar of the Americas, **La Citadelle** is North America's largest British-built fortress. After a failed American attack in 1775, the British erected a temporary citadel on the top of Cap Diamant. Inspired by the Fortifications of Vauban in France, La Citadelle's permanent star-shaped stone structure with five bastions was built from 1820 to 1831.

A guided visit (offered in French and English) is the only way to visit this active military base, home to Canada's sole French-speaking battalion, the Royal 22e Régiment. Book tickets online for the **one-hour tour** *(billets.lacitadelle.qc.ca/Online; adult/child/under 10 $22/8/free)*, followed by a self-guided exploration of the museum, covering centuries of military history with some 15,000 artifacts, including displays of weapons, flags and uniforms. The best time to go is on summer mornings at 10am from Wednesday to Sunday, when the regiment's band performs on the fortress parade ground.

MORE QUÉBEC CITY FESTIVALS

Festival d'été de Québec
MAP: 16 P129 E6

This 11-day music festival in July attracts over one-million spectators, who bop to the tunes of global and local artists at over 150 shows on stages across the city. *(feq.ca/en)*

Fête nationale du Québec
Also called St-Jean-Baptiste Day, and marking the start of summer, this June 24 celebration has transformed from pagan summer solstice festival to religious celebration to public holiday honoring Québécois culture with parties, music and fireworks. *(fetenationale.gouv.qc.ca)*

Igloofest
MAP: 17 P128 A1

For three days in March, internationally renowned DJs soundtrack an outdoor rave where Québécois step-touch in winter gear. *(quebec.igloofest.ca)*

Contemplate Contemporary Art
MUSEUMS AND INSTALLATIONS

MAP: 18 P129 H3

Eclectic and avant-garde, Québec City's fine-arts scene is full of surprises. Nonprofit arts foundation **EXMURO** (exmuro.com; free) curates an open-air summer program in Basse-Ville showcasing works by local and international artists. Expect quirky street performances and thought-provoking temporary installations; check the website to see where they're hiding. EXMURO's Place-Royale museum is open year-round. Stop by to see the **Museum of Bad Art** – a room packed with well-intentioned art gone awry.

To become a local art aficionado, reserve a couple hours for the **Musée National des beaux-arts du Québec** (mnbaq.org; adult/18-30/child $24/18/free). This Plaines d'Abraham museum spreads across several pavilions and holds the world's largest collection of Québécois art, covering colonial painting to contemporary sculptures. A new glass-walled pavilion dedicated to the work of 20th-century Québec painter Jean-Paul Riopelle is scheduled to open in the fall of 2026.

Honor the Courage of Irish Québec
RIVER ISLAND TOUR

MAP: 19 P129 H4

Set sail to Grosse-Île, a St Lawrence River island 48km east of Québec City, where Canada's immigration story takes a solemn turn. From 1832 to 1937, the island served as a quarantine station for newcomers entering the Port de Québec. Crosses mark the mass graves of nearly 7500 people buried here, including over 5000 people who perished in 1847 alone. Many of those lost in 1847 were Irish immigrants fleeing the Emerald Isle's potato famine on 'coffin ships' where they contracted typhus, leaving behind hundreds of orphans later adopted by French-Canadian families. Today, Grosse-Île is preserved as the **Irish Memorial National Historic Site** (parks.canada.ca/lhn-nhs/qc/grosseile)

 MARVELOUS MESS

The year: 1957. The town: Warwick, southwest of Québec City. A customer walks into restaurant Le Lutin Qui Rit and asks owner Fernand Lachance for cheese curds atop his fries. Lachance obliges, muttering it'll be a '*maudite poutine*' – a 'hell of a mess.' The name apparently stuck – and so did the snack. That's one of many poutine origin stories; others argue the name comes from pouding, French for pudding. Regardless, poutine spent the next half century climbing the culinary ladder from rural junk food to restaurant mainstay, sizzling as a source of Québec pride during February's **Semaine de la Poutine festival** (lapoutineweek.com).

where guided tours chronicle the heartbreak and resilience of those who passed through.

Visiting requires a boat ride. Book an excursion with **Croisières AML** (p135; *croisieres aml.com; from $74.99*) for a six-hour adventure, including a 35-minute ferry crossing each way and a guided tour of the island's landmarks. Back in Old Québec, a Celtic cross erected on Rue McMahon serves as a thanks from Ireland, honoring the city's compassion during the tumultuous famine years.

Sop Up City Views
OBSERVATORY AND SPA

Get to know Québec City's skyline from some of the best vantage points in town. First-time visitors will appreciate **Observatoire de la Capitale** (MAP: 20 P128 D5; *obser vatoire-capitale.com; adult/child $15/7*) – located on the 31st floor of Édifice Marie-Guyart, Québec City's tallest tower (132m), steps from the Assemblée nationale du Québec. Bring headphones and use the smartphone-friendly audio guide to learn about local history while taking in 360-degree views, including a clear shot of Old Québec jutting into the St Lawrence River. Your best bet is to buy same-day tickets: check 'Today's View' on the website to see if skies are clear. Timed tickets can be purchased online.

NEIGHBORHOODS BEYOND THE WALLS

St-Jean-Baptiste: A bohemian neighborhood within walking distance of the old city walls, its streets are lined with buzzy cafes and steep hills stacked with houses. Wander along Rue St-Jean, which becomes pedestrianized in summer.

St-Roch: Considered the hippest nabe in Québec City, Rue St-Joseph Est runs through it like an artery and **Église St-Roch** (the city's largest church) stands at its center.

Limoilou: Across the St Charles River, this 'hood gave birth to Québec hip-hop and is often referred to as 'up-and-coming'. Stylish cafes and restaurants can be found along Avenue 3e.

For a relaxing experience, try **SkySpa** (MAP: 21 P128 C6; *skyspa. ca; from $45*), located on the 17th floor of the Complexe Jules-Dallaire in Ste-Foy. Guests can follow a Scandinavian-style thermal circuit (sauna, cold plunge, relaxation spaces) and end in an outdoor pool overlooking Québec City. Bring a bathing suit and flip-flops; bathrobes and towels are provided. Views are particularly wow-worthy around sunset.

Maison de la littérature

Leaf Through Québec City's Loveliest Libraries ARCHITECTURE AND TOURS

Word nerds and design buffs both agree: Québec City's libraries are luminous. Start by peeking inside the **Maison de la littérature** (MAP: 22 P129 E3; *maisondela litterature.qc.ca; free*), a 19th-century neo-Gothic church now serving as epicenter for the preservation of French literature in Québec City. Sun pours through the towering triple lancet windows, spotlighting the minimalist white interior packed with books by French and Québécois authors. It's a peaceful place to take a break from Old Québec's bustle. It's closed Mondays.

Across the street is the **Morrin Centre** (MAP: 23 P129 F3; *morrin.org/en; $5*) – a former jail transformed into an English-language community hub. Most visitors come here for a **one-hour tour** of the spooky basement jail cells *($18.50)*, where prisoners etched graffiti into the floor. The Victorian-style library is also worth a gander, with over 27,000 books lining wooden shelves and a balcony edged in cast-iron railings. Check the website for English-language events like poetry readings, history lectures and lessons in teatime etiquette. It's closed to visitors on Mondays and Tuesdays.

LISTINGS

Best Places for...

$ Budget $$ Midrange $$$ Top End

See p128 for map of locations

EXPLORE QUÉBEC CITY

Eating

Coffee & Pastries

La Maison Smith $
24 G3
'Smith Café's' locally roasted coffee, flaky croissants and nibbles are best enjoyed on the patio on historic Place-Royale. *smithcafe.com, 7am-7pm Sun-Wed, to 8pm Thu-Sat*

Café Apotek $
25 F2
This minimalist Nordic-style boulangerie-cafe serves high-quality, small-batch coffee and artfully-crafted desserts in the Old Port. *@apotek.bakery, 8am-4pm Mon-Fri, 8am-5pm Sat, 9am-5pm Sun*

Breakfast & Brunch

Le Billig $
26 C4
Searching for crêpes? Get yours at this popular food tour destination, known for having some of Québec City's best. Order yours savory or sweet. *@lebilligcreperiebistro, 11am-10pm*

Le Hobbit $$
27 D4
Drop by this French-style St-Jean-Baptiste bistro – tiny and cozy, like the Tolkien character its name suggests – serving a splendid gourmet croque madame and salmon gravlax. *lehobbit.com, 8am-10pm*

Café du Monde $$
28 H2
Drop into this classic French bistro next to the cruise terminal for fancy omelets, eggs Benny and river views. *lecafedumonde.com, 11:30am-9:30pm Mon-Fri, at 9am Sat & Sun*

Plates of Poutine

Le Chic Shack $$
29 G3
Gourmet poutine with hand-smashed potatoes is the name of the game at this ode to all things greasy. Try La Forestière (poutine topped with a mushroom ragout), washed down with a boozy milkshake. *lechicshack.ca, 8am-9pm*

Chez Gaston $
30 A3
St-Roch might be the epicenter of Québec City cool, but the kids still like to keep it classic at this traditional *casse-croûte* (snack shack) with a mean poutine. *chezgaston quebec.ca, 11am-9pm Sun-Thu, to 10pm Fri & Sat*

Québécois Cuisine

Aux Anciens Canadiens $$$
31 F3
Dine on *tourtière* (meat pie), wild game, pea soup and other house classics in the oldest house in Québec City, constructed in the 1670s. *auxancienscanadiens.qc.ca, noon-10:30pm*

La Bûche $$
32 F4
Can't make it to a rural sugar shack? Visit this urban alternative, serving *pâté chinois* (a Québécois shepherd's pie), deer tartare and smoked trout. *restolabuche.com, 8am-9:30pm Sun-Wed, to 10pm Thu-Sat*

143

International Flavors

Le Don 💲💲

33 G2

The heaping plates of globally inspired, plant-based food at Québec's first vegan restaurant ensure no one goes hungry – not even carnivores. *donresto.com, 11am-9pm Mon-Thu, to 10pm Fri, hours vary Sat & Sun*

Bati Cantine 💲💲

34 A3

This casual dining option in St-Roch serves classic Thai and Cambodian foods like Khmer noodles and tom yum soup. *cantinebati.com, hours vary*

French Dinners in Old Québec

Lapin Sauté 💲💲

35 G4

Rabbit is the star at this charming French spot in Petit-Champlain, also known for its duck and seafood cassoulet. *lapinsaute.com, 11:30am-9:30pm*

Chez Temporel 💲💲

36 F2

Reserve a table to enjoy dinner at this artists' cafe turned French bistro tucked down a quiet street in Haute-Ville, open since 1974. *cheztemporel.com, 11am-9pm*

Drinking

Heavenly Hot Chocolate

Érico

37 C4

Indulge in a 'decadent' cup of *chocolat chaud* – a super-rich blend of seven chocolates – at this St-Jean-Baptiste chocolaterie with a connected chocolate museum. *ericochocolatier.com, 10:30am-9pm, from 11am Sun*

Le Petit Dep

38 G3

It's tough choosing between regular *chocolat chaud* and the festive blend (with homemade raspberry marshmallows) at this charming cafe-cum-*dépanneur*. *lepetitdep.com/quebec, 8am-6pm Mon-Thu, to 8pm Fri-Sun*

Craft Beer & Microbreweries

L'Oncle Antoine

39 H3

This stone cavern in Place-Royale housed the first woman-owned business in Québec (1754). Cheers the business-savvy lady with a shot of maple whiskey. *@pub loncleantoine, 11am-1am*

La Korrigane

40 A3

The owner of this St-Roch microbrewery crafts her small-batch beers using Québécois products. *korrigane.ca, 11:30am-midnight Sun-Thu, to 2am Fri & Sat*

Speakeasies & Craft Cocktails

Justine

41 E2

Look for windows covered with black curtains near the train station to find this undercover lounge with great music, food and cocktails. *@justinespeakeasy, 6pm-3am Wed-Sun*

JJacques

42 A3

Named one of the 50 best bars in Canada, this St-Roch speakeasy is equal parts seafood bar, dinner restaurant and cocktail club. *jjacques.ca, 5pm-1am Sun-Thu, to 3am Fri & Sat*

St-Jean-Baptiste's Best Bars

Le Drague

43 D4

This LGBTIQ+ bar in Québec City features multiple dance floors, glittery performances and weekend drag brunch where all (of legal age) are

welcome. *ledrague.com, 11am-3am*

Le Projet
 C4

Look up at this gastropub's ornate vaulted ceilings while nursing one of the 29 microbrews on tap. *publeprojet.com, 3pm-1am Mon-Wed, 11am-3am Thu-Sat, 1am Sun*

Le Sacrilège
45 C4

In summer, it would be sacrilege to miss sitting on the spacious hidden terrace while sipping Québec craft beer. *barlesacrilege.com, noon-3am*

Shopping

Antiques & Ornaments
Antiquités Bolduc
46 G2

Open the moss-green door anchoring a stretch of Rue St-Paul appropriately dubbed 'Antiquities Row' to find a forest of 19th- and 20th-century treasures. *lesantiquitesbolduc.com, 10am-5pm Mon-Fri, from 10:30am Sat*

G & M Bourguet Antiquités
47 G2

A lovely father-and-son-run antique shop with Québec antiques, folk art, carved wooden pieces and furniture. *gmbourguet.com, 10:30am-noon & 1:30-5pm Mon-Sat*

Boutique de Noël
48 G3

It's always Christmas in this kitsch-tastic boutique decked out in holiday lights and Québec-themed ornaments, even in summer, near the Notre-Dame basilica. *boutiquedenoel.ca, 9am-11pm*

Indigenous Art
Galerie d'art Inuit Brousseau
49 F4

Admire intricate Inuit soapstone and basalt carvings by artists from Arctic Canada in this museum-caliber gallery. *artinuitbrousseau.ca, 9:30am-5:30pm*

Éditions Galerie l'Imagerie
50 H3

This little shop sells prints, paintings and puzzles with images of Québec by Québec artists. *egiclees.com, 11am-4pm Mon-Fri, from noon Sat & Sun*

Hand-crafted & Tailored
Artisans Canada
51 F3

This family-run emporium initially opened as a furniture store in 1946; it now showcases Canadian-made art, clothing, jewelry and quality souvenirs. *artisanscanada.com, 9am-9pm*

Coeur de Loup
52 A4

Local fashion designer Nathalie Jourdain makes women's clothing to order at her atelier on Rue St-Vallier Est. *coeurdeloup.ca, 11am-5pm Wed-Fri*

Nature's Candies
Le Grand Marché
53 A1

Planning a picnic? Splurge on Québec cheeses, fruits, charcuterie and fresh baguettes at this two-floor farmers market in Limoilou. *legrandmarchedequebec.com, 9am-6pm Mon-Fri, to 5pm Sat & Sun*

La Petite Cabane à sucre du Québec
54 G4

Everything at the 'Little Québec Sugar Shack' is marvelously mapled: candy, popcorn, butter, sugar, all sold alongside bottles of the sweet nectar itself. *petitecabane.com, 10am-9:30pm*

EXPLORE

QUÉBEC CITY

⭐ WORTH A TRIP

Île d'Orléans

Rural Île d'Orléans, 15km upstream from Québec City, is a pastoral paradise of riverside villages, vineyards and fruit farms rolling toward the St Lawrence. The 34km-long and 8km-wide island can easily be explored by car in a day, though its serene charms may inspire staying longer.

GETTING THERE
This trip is best with a car: drive clockwise around the island along Chemin Royal, starting at the visitors, center and ending with a trip to the island's wineries.

Scan the QR code to visit the official tourism website of Île d'Orléans.

Admire Architecture

St-Jean is the best preserved village on Île-d'Orléans, with 19th-century cottages (pictured) stretching along the southeastern shore. It's anchored by **Église St-Jean** a stately stone church and cemetery from the 1730s. St-Jean's crown jewel is the **Manoir Mauvide-Genest** (*manoir mauvidegenest.com; closed Tue & Wed; adult/child $10.50/free*), an archetypal French mansion built in 1752. Costumed interpreters guide visitors through the house, using period furniture and household items to illustrate upper-class living in New France.

Dive into History

For an interactive crash course on the St Lawrence River's nautical past, drop by the **Musée Maritime de L'Île d'Orléans** (*museemaritimeio.ca/en; Jun–mid-Oct; adult/child $12/free*). The property is based on a former shipyard. One of its buildings is a rowboat workshop from 1837; stone trenches in the ground mark where vessels were once assembled. Visitors can get an up-close look at antique tools and an ocean-blue tugboat from 1934.

DELPIXEL/SHUTTERSTOCK

Savor Wine & Chocolate

Though farmers didn't start cultivating wine-centric grapes here until the 1980s, Île d'Orléans is now a Canadian vin-topia. **Vignoble Isle de Bacchus** *(isledebacchus.com; 10am-6pm)* is one of the island's viticulture pioneers, with 11 hectares of vines overlooking the river. Tour the grounds and taste everything from dry reds to sparkling wines, all made on site, and stop by more island vineyards along main road Chemin Royal.

Head 6km west of the vineyard to indulge at **Chocolaterie de l'Île d'Orléans** *(chocolaterieorleans.com; 9am-6pm)* selling everything from pralines and maple candy to figures shaped like chocolate moose (get it?) Bonus – the chocolaterie sits on the island's western tip, with an unobstructed Québec City view.

TAKE A BREAK
Plop onto a Victorian sofa for a tea tasting *($25)*, plus scones and petit fours *($27)*, at **La Maison de Thé** *(lamaisondethe.com; 11am-5pm Thu-Sun)*.

★ WORTH A TRIP

Parc de la Chute-Montmorency

Head 12km east of Old Québec to see the Montmorency River plunge 83m before emptying into the raging St Lawrence in **Parc de la Chute-Montmorency**. The chute, or waterfall, is 30m taller than Niagara Falls, veiling this park's surrounding sandstone and shale cliffs in a nimbus of mist – worth a half-day adventure.

GETTING THERE
No car? Reach the park via bicycle (follow Corridor du Littoral, p139). public bus 800 toward Beauport or with **Unitours** (toursvieuxquebec. com; adult/child $29/20).

Scenic Strolls
Most journeys begin in a parking lot – one at the foot of the falls and another above. From the lower lot, paved trails and rocky banks trace a horseshoe around the rainbow-wreathed water, leading to a long staircase that zigzags over 480 steps to the top of the falls. Once above, you can cross a 23m-long suspension bridge, which spans the top of the falls and provides a bird's-eye view of the plummeting water. If you'd prefer to avoid the long climbs, ride the scenic **cable car** between the upper and lower lot *(closed early Nov-late Dec; $14.95 for unlimited same-day trips)*.

High-octane Activities
For a close-up view of the powerful cascade, consider fastening on a helmet, hooking yourself to a cable and soaring 300m across the Montmorency canyon. The **zip line** *(sepaq.com; Jun-mid-Oct; adult/child $32/24)* is strung between two raised wooden platforms, and everything in between is crashing water and open air, affording you the closest possible view of the falls. Even better, this zip line has two separate cables, allowing you to ride alongside – or even race – a second person. The ride lasts less than a minute, and you only cross once; visitors should still

Scan the QR code for entrance fees and opening hours.

CK-TRAVELPHOTOS/SHUTTERSTOCK

budget for about 30 minutes for the full experience, including up to 10 minutes to walk back from the opposite side of the river. Riders must be at least 15 years of age and weigh between 41kg (90lbs) and 99kg (218lbs). Book tickets through the main Sépaq website.

The upper park is currently undergoing a revitalization project, which includes a full replacement of a via ferrata climbing route – where daredevils clip onto steel cables and navigate a cliffside route of iron rungs.

For winter fun, try your hand at ice climbing the waterfall's frozen cliffs with **Aventurex** *(aventurex.ca; $154, ages 14 and up)*. Guides provide equipment and lessons for everyone from beginners to ice-axe aficionados. Budget for five hours.

TAKE A BREAK
Enjoy burgers or salads on the scenic terrace in front of **Manoir Montmorency** *(hours vary by season)*, a replica of an 18th-century governor's residence near the upper entrance.

★ WORTH A TRIP

Wendake

Deep in Québec City's western suburbs, Wendake's 2000-plus residents are descended from the Wendat (also known as the Huron-Wendat) who once dominated this region. Examine Québec's Indigenous heritage on a tour of exhibits along the wooded banks of the Akiawenrahk River, also called the St Charles.

GETTING THERE
Wendake is a 30-minute drive from Québec City. With no car, hop on a public bus; budget for one hour for the journey. Plan on spending half a day here.

Meet the Wendat

Wendake's centerpiece is the **Musée Huron-Wendat** *(museehuronwendat.ca; adult/youth $18/9)*, part of the impressive **Hôtel-Musée Premières Nations** *(First Nations Hotel-Museum; hotelpremieresnations.ca)*. Choose a 90-minute guided or audio tour to learn about the Wendats' ancestral territories, the upheaval of colonialism and Wendake's current tribal government.

Outside, take the main path to the **Ekionkiestha' National Longhouse** *(adult/youth $13/6.50)*, a full-sized replica of the dwellings the Wendat would have built in the centuries before European influence. Gas-lit flames burn in simulated fire pits, and the interior is adorned with skins and drying vegetables. Within a protective timber wall, guides describe the architecture and give an account of daily life in a Wendat village. To fully embrace the experience, you can actually bed down in the longhouse – for a cool $645 per night.

Powerful Waters

Walk five minutes from the Hôtel-Musée Premières Nations parking lot to see **Kabir Kouba Waterfall** as it slides gently down a sedimentary rock face, descending 28m into a narrow canyon. This part of the Akiawenrahk River has a

Scan the QR code to learn more about the Musée Huron-Wendat.

ANNE RICHARD/SHUTTERSTOCK

powerful current, so swimming isn't recommended. A little further downstream, though, you'll find **Canots Légaré** (*canotslegare.com; mid-May–mid-Oct; from $17*), a boathouse renting canoes, kayaks and stand-up paddleboards. Follow the same watery routes Wendat fishers took in generations past.

Walk Through Legends

Onhwa' Lumina (*onhwalumina.ca; adult/child $34/18*) is an immersive nighttime experience that uses lyrical recorded narration, sophisticated lighting effects and information panels to describe the cosmology of the Wendat. Follow a trail through elaborate sets and cinematic projections for a magical, family-friendly excursion into the forest.

DINING PICK
Sample upscale Indigenous-inspired cuisine at **Restaurant La Traite** (*restaurantlatraite.ca; 7:30am-9:30pm; $$$*) in the Hôtel-Musée Premières Nations.

Montréal & Québec City Toolkit

Family Travel	154
Accommodations	155
Food, Drink & Nightlife	156
LGBTIQ+ Travelers	158
Health & Safe Travel	159
Responsible Travel	160
Accessible Travel	162
Nuts & Bolts	163
Language	164

Belvédère Kondiaronk (p90), Montréal
AWANA JF/SHUTTERSTOCK

Family Travel

Budding scientists, fussy foodies, artsy adolescents and tomorrow's ice hockey pros: Montréal's action-packed playland is as varied as the seasons, catering to children with all types of tastes. Everyone's going to need a nap.

Québec Cuisine

Picky palates will love Québécois comfort food. Bite into bagels at legendary **St-Viateur** (p108), choose from 30 styles of poutine at **La Banquise** (p97) and order hot dogs from the century-old **Montréal Pool Room** (p70). Prefer sweets? Don't miss the *cabane à sucre* at **Place Jacques-Cartier** (p43), everything smothered in maple syrup.

Kids in Québec City

Wander through **Musée de la Civilisation**'s (p131) interactive, kid-geared exhibits. Celebrate winter by gliding around **Place d'Youville**'s (p137) ice-skating rink and pick up speed while tobogganing down the **Glissade de la Terrasse** (p138). In summer, venture to **Parc de la Chute-Montmorency** (p148), where a zip line zooms past a 83m waterfall.

Make History Fun

At Montréal's **Pointe-à-Callière** (p44) museum, children can play archaeologist and learn about St Lawrence River pirates.

OUTSIDE IN SUMMER

Beat the heat by bouncing around Aquazilla at **Plage Jean-Doré** (p51), climb the Old Ports' **Voiles en Voiles** (p41) ropes course or run around the green fields surrounding **Lac aux Castors** (p90).

Winter Wonderland

Tube down **Parc du Mont-Royal**'s (p90) slopes, skate **Parc Jean-Drapeau**'s (p50) forest trail or build snow people. It's free.

Montréal Museum Discounts

Save on **Espace pour la vie**'s immersive museums (Biodôme, Insectarium, Planétarium, Jardin Botanique and Biosphère, p76–9) with a **MULTI Passport**, covering two adults and three children for $149. Passports last for 12 months.

BONCHAN/SHUTTERSTOCK

Accommodations

Forgo big-name chains – Québec is replete with boutique hotels and B&Bs. Winter rates are lower; summer stays pricier.

Where to Stay if You Love...

 Art & Architecture
Downtown (p55) Magnificent museums, 19th-century mansions and renowned performing arts venues anchor this centrally-located neighborhood.

Stylish Streets & Pretty Parks
Plateau Mont-Royal (p87) Crafty boutiques, cocktail bars and cafes line blocks enlivened by murals. Leafy Parc du Mont-Royal and Parc La Fontaine bookend walkable thoroughfares.

Artsy Aesthetics & Global Tastes
Mile End (p101) New-wave and old-school restaurants mix with wine bars, breweries and creative clothing stores between Plateau Mont-Royal and foodie destination Little Italy.

 Nightlife & LGBTIQ+ Culture
Quartier Latin & the Village (p73) Microbreweries line Rue St-Denis and rainbow flags decorate Rue Ste-Catherine, heart of the gayborhood.

 Old Europe Ambiance
Québec City (p127) French Canada's crown jewel blends contemporary culture with its colonial Old Town, fortified by medieval-style ramparts.

HOW MUCH FOR A NIGHT

Hostel **$30–150**

Midrange B&B **$150–300**

High-end boutique hotel **Over $250**

OUR PICK ★
We Love to Stay in...
Old Montréal (p35) This is where to find charming boutique hotels. Montréal first took shape here, and it continues to be the best place to get acquainted with the city, offering atmospheric plazas lined with soaring cathedrals and the action-packed Old Port.

Food, Drink & Nightlife

Allergies & Intolerances

Those who need to watch what they eat have plenty of options in Montréal and Québec City. Always communicate dietary restrictions to your server.

HOW TO SAY...

I'm allergic... Je suis allergique...

to gluten au gluten

to nuts aux noix

to seafood aux fruits de mer

I'm lactose intolerant Je suis intolérant(e) au lactose

I'm vegetarian/vegan Je suis végétarien(ne)/végane

MENU DECODER

Carte
Menu

Table d'hôte
A prix-fixe menu with several courses

Apportez votre vin
'Bring your own wine' – the restaurant doesn't serve alcohol but will uncork guests'.

CASSE-CROÛTES

The term casse-croûte translates as 'snack' but it's also a food joint, be it a rural roadside shack or a late-night corner spot in cities. It's the greasy-spoon sister of a canteen and the mother of a modern fast-food counter, serving Québec specialties like poutine and US-inspired classics like burgers.

Bistros, Brasseries & Buvettes

Bistros are casual, cozy, French-inspired spots with moderately priced food and wine. Brasseries (literally 'breweries') are generally larger, serving beer and hearty meals, while microbrasseries are actual breweries. Buvettes are wine-centric bars with shareable plates.

HOW TO... Pay the Bill

Getting the bill Asking for the bill in French? Say, '*la facture, s'il vous plaît.*' This is different from European French, where diners ask for *l'addition*. Tongue-tied? Many servers speak English.

Payment Most restaurants will present you with a portable credit-card machine, where you can easily split the bill and choose your tip amount.

Tipping The tip (*pourboire* or *service* in French) isn't included on restaurant bills. Add 15% as the standard; more for exceptional service. Based on a law introduced in 2025, percentage options must be calculated before Québec's sales tax is added.

PRICE RANGES

The following price ranges refer to the average cost of a main course.

$ less than $18
$$ $18 to $28
$$$ over $28

OPENING HOURS

Cafes 8am to 4pm; some close 6pm
Restaurants 7am (breakfast) to 10pm (dinner)
Bars 5pm to midnight or later
Clubs 10pm to 3am on weekends

GLYN THOMAS/ALAMY

Going Out

Timing A night in Québec's two principal cities typically starts with a post-work gathering beginning at 5pm and perhaps followed by dinner, cocktails, a live performance or dancing till dawn. Weeknights last until midnight or 1am, while weekends rage until 3am and beyond, with Montréalers partying later than the rest of the province.

Montréal's offerings Electronic music is particularly popular here, where DJs spin everywhere from pseudo-speakeasies (try **Sans Soleil** (p69) – line up outside the door) to high-capacity clubs (try **Stereo** (p85) – buy tickets online in advance). Get ready for late nights: parties usually pick up steam around midnight and can pulse until morning. Prefer daytime revelry? Attend one of the province's seasonal outdoor events, like **Piknic Électronik** (p50), a Sunday shindig from May to October where Montréalers dance beneath the setting sun.

HOW MUCH FOR A…

Shot of espresso
$3.25

Pint of beer (16oz)
$5–10

Craft cocktail
$12–20

Plain bagel
$1.20

Plate of poutine
$10

Smoked-meat sandwich
$15

Three-course meal at a top-rated restaurant
$60–100

LGBTIQ+ Travelers

Montréal is home to one of North America's largest LGBTIQ+ neighborhoods, the Village. Québec City's scene is small but spirited.

Beyond Montréal's Village

Queer-friendly Spaces The Village's Rue Ste-Catherine is central to MTL's **LGBTIQ+ nightlife** (p85), but it's not the only pink-waving neighborhood. In the Plateau, wake up to drag brunch at **Robin des Bois** (p95) and visit Villeray to clink wine glasses with queer couples at **Polari** (p112). You'll find more LGBTIQ-welcoming hangouts in Little Italy and Mile End.

Pop-up Parties Check out these parties off the Village's main drag. Homopop's **West End Gays** (*@homopop_*) is a magnet for dancing to pop and disco, **Queen & Queer** (*@queenqueermtl*) throws Sapphic soirées at various venues, **Ballroom 4 Community** (*@ballroom4community*) presents vogue-centric shows, DJ **Reid Bourgeois** *(reidbourgeois.com)* plays parties for a devout gay crowd and **ElleLui** (*elleluimtl.com*) promotes trans joy on the dance floor.

By Day of the Week

MONDAY: Saloon (p85) Dine on the terrace.
TUESDAY: Polari (p112) Share a wine bottle.
WEDNESDAY: Aigle Noir (p85) Down brews; wear leather.
THURSDAY: Renard (p85) Dance off dinner.
FRIDAY: Cabaret Mado (p82) Applaud drag icon Mado.
SATURDAY: Stereo (p85) Sashay till sunrise.
SUNDAY: Stud (p85) Disco with the daddies.

QUEER IN QC

Most of Québec City's LGBTIQ+ scene hugs Rue St-Jean within the St-Jean-Baptiste neighborhood. **Le Drague** (p144) is the epicenter for dancing and drag.

LGBTIQ+ WALKING TOUR

Scan this QR code to book Thom Seivewright's LGBTIQ+ history walking tour through Downtown Montréal's rainbow-hued past.

Resources

- **Montréal Pride** Info on the largest LGBTIQ+ event in the French-speaking world. *fiertemontreal.com*
- **queermtl.tumblr.com** Find LGBTIQ+ events throughout Montréal.
- **Fugues** Catch up on Québec's latest queer news. *fugues.com*
- **Fierté de Québec.ca** Get ready for Québec City's Pride. *fiertedequebec.ca*

Health & Safe Travel

Québec is a relatively safe destination – but it's still prudent to stay alert and follow local laws while exploring.

KILLER COLD

Québec's winter temperatures can drop below -30°C. Avoid life-threatening cold-related ailments by wearing warm layers and covering all body surfaces, including ears and fingers. Watch for the 'umbles' (stumbles, mumbles, fumbles and grumbles), symptoms of impending hypothermia.

Health Insurance & Medication

Canada might be praised for its taxpayer-funded healthcare system, but unless you're a Canadian citizen, it's not possible to take advantage of the program. If your regular health insurance policy doesn't cover you abroad, consider purchasing travel insurance to help fund any necessary medical care or prescription drugs while visiting. Paying out of pocket can be costly. If you need over-the-counter medicine, search for big pharmacy chains like **Jean Coutu** *(jeancoutu.com)* and **Pharmaprix** *(pharmaprix.ca)*.

Tap Is Tops

It's safe to drink tap water in both cities – most H_2O comes filtered from the St Lawrence River.

QUICK INFO

Bike Security
Always secure bicycle rentals with a lock.

Public Transit
Montréal's Métro is generally safe, but it's wise to safeguard personal belongings.

Road Rules
It's illegal to turn right on a red light in Montréal.

Cannabis & Alcohol

Marijuana is legal to purchase and consume for people ages 21 and up. It's illegal to smoke in public. All cannabis must be bought at a Société Québécoise du Cannabis store *(SQDC; sqdc.ca)*. The legal drinking age in Québec is 18. The primary place to buy alcohol is at an SAQ outlet *(saq.com)*.

--- **GET A GARAGE** ---

Due to increased car theft around Montréal since 2021, it's wise to park in a garage overnight. Cars with foreign registrations are occasionally targeted.

Responsible Travel

Follow these tips to leave a lighter footprint, support local and have a positive impact on communities.

Ride, Roll & Stroll

Minimize your carbon footprint by choosing alternatives to cars. Hop on Montréal's Métro: it's a reliable way to chug between neighborhoods. Join a bikeshare program: Montréal's BIXI and Québec City's àVélo make it easy to see the sites on wheels. Hop on a boat: book a Montréal river tour with **Le Petit Navire's** (p46) electric fleet. Hoof it: both cities are pedestrian-friendly.

Choose Green Stays

Sleep soundly at Green Key–certified, eco-conscious hotels. Try Montréal's **Le Mount Stephen** *(lemountstephen.com)*, a 19th-century mansion modernized for contemporary tastes, or **Hôtel de l'ITHQ** *(ithq.qc.ca)*, run by hospitality students.

OUR PICK ★

Get a Guide

No one knows how to treat their town better than Québec's licensed tour guides. Decode Montréal with help from in-the-know experts **Spade & Palacio** (p92).

Sustainable Shopping

Montréal and Québec City are all about repurposed vintage and lightly used antiques. In Montréal, hunt for rehabbed denim at **La Caravane Vintage** (p99) and restored leather at **Palmo Goods** (p99). In Québec City, stalk shops along Rue St-Paul, an 'antiques alley' packed with stores like **Antiquités Bolduc** (p145).

Resources

- **mtl.org** Tourismé Montréal offers sustainable travel ideas.
- **quebec-cite.com** Québec City's tourism site suggests how to be a responsible visitor.

HONOR INDIGENOUS CULTURE

The original stewards of America's landscape hold keys to protecting its ecology. Learn about their Earth-savvy lifestyles at Montréal's **Musée McCord Stewart** (p66) and Wendake's **Musée Huron-Wendat** (p150).

Favor Farmers Markets

Support local producers and artisans by visiting farmers markets. More than 300 stands fill Montréal's **Marché Jean-Talon** (p110) and more than 100 Canadian producers sell treats at Québec City's **Le Grand Marché** (p145). Champion eateries that reduce, reuse or eliminate waste, like Montréal's **Café des Habitudes** (p112), almost entirely decorated in secondhand furniture.

GET EDUCATED

Visit Montréal's Biosphère to learn more about environmental issues impacting our planet and how to address them. Immersive, hands-on exhibits appeal to kids. Scan the QR code for tickets.

Climate Change & Travel

It's impossible to ignore the impact we have when traveling; Lonely Planet urges all travelers to engage with their travel carbon footprint, which will mainly come from air travel. While there often isn't an alternative, travelers can look to minimize the number of flights they take, opt for newer aircraft and use cleaner ground transport, such as trains. One proposed solution – purchasing carbon offsets – unfortunately does not cancel out the impact of individual flights. While most destinations will depend on air travel for the foreseeable future, for now, pursuing ground-based travel where possible is the best course of action.

The **UN Carbon Offset Calculator** shows how flying impacts a household's emissions.

The **ICAO's carbon emissions calculator** allows visitors to analyze the CO2 generated by point-to-point journeys.

Accessible Travel

Sensory-friendly Fun & Discounts
In Montréal, travelers with sensory sensitivities enjoy 'peaceful mornings' at **Centre des Sciences de Montréal** (p41), relaxed performances at **TOHU** (p109), and sensory kits at **Espace pour la vie** museums. At some museums, including QC's **Musée de la Civilisation** (p131), disabled visitors and companions enter gratis.

Plates Without Peeking
Find out what it's like to dine sans sight at Montréal's **Onoir** *(onoir.com)*, where blind and low-vision waitstaff serve meals in darkened rooms. A percentage of profits goes to local associations supporting the blind community.

Representation matters. That's what makes the exhibits at Montréal's **MEM** (p66; Centre des mémoires montréalaises) so spectacular. This museum embraces stories from a diversity of Montréalers, including disability activist and wheelchair user Maude Massicotte, filmed navigating Montréal in a mini documentary for permanent exhibition **Montréal**. Inclusivity doesn't end there: MEM assures mobility, hearing and visual accommodations are available throughout the museum, and offers educational programming all about accessibility. You might even be greeted by a disabled docent.

TRY A TAXI
Many public bus lines accommodate wheelchair users, but ramps can occasionally be out of order. Instead, call Montréal's **Taxi Para-Adapté** *(taxiparaadapte.ca)* and Québec City's **Transport Accessible du Québec** *(taq.qc.ca)*.

Accommodations
Modern hotels incorporate access into their designs, but hotels constructed before the 1990s may lack certain mobility-access features like elevators and ramps. Check before booking.

--- MONTRÉAL'S MÉTRO ---

Roughly 30 of the city's 68 Métro stations have elevators, making over half the system ill-equipped for travelers with reduced mobility. Visit *stm.info* for a map of accessible stations.

Resources
- **keroul.qc.ca** Kéroul creates accessible travel itineraries for people with limited mobility.
- **aqepa.org/courslsq** Learn LSQ, Québec's primary sign language.

Nuts & Bolts

Opening Hours
Hours remain consistent year-round, though outdoor tour companies generally operate seasonally.

Restaurants
Breakfast 7-11am, lunch 11:30am-2:30pm, dinner 5-10pm, weekend brunch 10:30am-3pm

Bars and pubs Bars 5pm-midnight or later; pubs with food open around noon.

Museums 10am-5pm; most close Monday and some stay open late for one day, typically mid-week

Shops 11am-6pm

Grocery stores 8am-10pm

Ouvert Open
Fermé Closed

QUICK INFO
Time zone Eastern Time (EST/EDT; UTC/GMT minus five hours)
Country calling code +1
Emergency number 911
Population 9.1 million (all of Québec)

ELECTRICITY
Type A 120V/60Hz;
Type B 120V/60Hz

Measures & Weights
Québec uses the metric system, though many Canadians use a mix of metric and imperial measurements. Still, distance is measured in kilometers (1.6km equals 1 mile), speeds are in kilometers per hour (100km/h equals 62mph), gas is in liters (3.75L equals 1 US gallon) and weight is in grams.

Public Holidays
Québec observes eight statutory holidays. Select businesses remain open but hours are subject to change. Expect packed venues and higher hotel prices.

New Year's Day January 1

Good Friday and Easter Monday Late March to mid-April

Victoria Day The penultimate Monday in May (before the 25th)

National Indigenous Peoples Day (non-statutory) June 21

Fête Nationale du Québec (St-Jean-Baptiste Day) June 24

Canada Day July 1

Labour Day First Monday in September

Canadian Thanksgiving Second Monday in October

Remembrance Day (non-statutory) November 11

Christmas Day December 25

Language

French basics

Hello.
Bonjour. *bon·zhoor*

Goodbye.
Au revoir. *o·rer·vwa*

Excuse me.
Excusez-moi. *ek·skew·zay·mwa*

Sorry.
Pardon. *par·don*

Yes/no.
Oui/non. *wee/non*

Please.
S'il vous plaît. *seel voo play*

Thank you.
Merci. *mair·see*

Where's…?
Où est…? *Oo ay…?*

Fast phrases

Do you have any rooms available? Est-ce que vous avez des chambres libres? *es·ker voo za·vay day shom·brer lee·brer*

How much is it per night/person? Quel est le prix par nuit/personne? *kel ay ler pree par nwee/per·son*

I'd like to buy… Je voudrais acheter… *zher voo·dray ash·tay…*

Do you speak English? Parlez-vous anglais? *par·lay·voo ong·glay*

I'd like to reserve a table for… Je voudrais réserver une table pour… *zher voo·dray ray·zair·vay ewn ta·bler poor…*

What time is it? Y'est quelle heure? *il ay kel er*

It's (eight) o'clock. Il est (huit) heures. *il ay (weet) er*

Leave me alone! Fichez-moi la paix! *fee·shay·mwa lapay*

I'm ill. Je suis malade. *zher swee ma·lad*

I'm lost. Je suis perdu/perdue. *zhe swee·pair·dew (m/f)*

I'm allergic (to..). Je suis allergique (à …). *zher swee za·lair·zheek (a…)*

Call a doctor. Appelez un médecin. *a·play un mayd·sun*

Call the police. Appelez la police. *a·play la po·lees*

Numbers

 un *un*  **deux** *der*   **trois** *trwa*   **quatre** *cat*   **cinq** *sangk*

Québéc-quoi?!

There are some key differences between European French and the Québec version (known as 'Québécois' or *joual*). For example, while standard French for 'What time is it?' is *Quelle heure est-il?*, in Québec you're likely to hear *Y'est quelle heure?* instead. Other differences worth remembering are the terms for breakfast, lunch and dinner: rather than *petit déjeuner*, *déjeuner* and *dîner* you're likely to see and hear *déjeuner*, *dîner* and *souper*.

ENGLISH DONATIONS TO QUÉBÉCOIS

Québec French employs a lot of English words; eg English terms are generally used for car parts – even the word char (pronounced 'shar') for car may be heard.

Signs
Entrée Entrance
Femmes Women
Fermé Closed
Hommes Men
Ouvert Open
Renseignements Information
Sortie Exit
Toilettes/WC Toilets

Header

The sounds used in spoken French can almost all be found in English. If you read our pronunciation guides as if they were English, you'll be understood. There are a couple of exceptions: nasal vowels (represented in our guides by o or u followed by an almost inaudible nasal consonant sound m, n or ng), the 'funny' u (ew in our guides) and the deep-in-the-throat r. Syllables in French words are, for the most part, equally stressed. As English speakers tend to stress the first syllable, try adding a light stress on the final syllable of French words to compensate.

DATES AND TIMES

Afternoon après-midi *a-pray-mee-dee*
Evening soir *swar*
Night nuit *nwee*
Today aujourd'hui *o-zhoor-dwee*
Yesterday hier *yair*
Tomorrow demain *der-mun*

six *sees*   **sept** *set*   **huit** *weet*   **neuf** *nerf*   **dix** *dees*

Index

Sights p000   Map pages p000

See also separate subindexes for:
- Eating p169
- Drinking p170
- Shopping p171

A

accessible travel 27, 162
accommodations 155
activities 22–3, *see also individual activities*
air travel 24
amusement & adventure parks
  La Ronde 52
  Voiles en Voiles 41
architecture 12
Arsenal Art Contemporain 119
art 10, *see also individual galleries*
Assemblée nationale du Québec 136
Ave Duluth 95

B

B&Bs 155
bagels 108
ballet 64
bars, *see Drinking subindex*
basilicas, *see churches, chapels & basilicas*
Basilique Notre-Dame 38
Basilique-Cathédrale Notre-Dame-de-Québec 137
Batterie Royale 133
beaches & *plages*
  Plage de l'Horloge 39
  Plage Jean-Doré 51
  Plage de Verdun 122
bicycle rentals 53, 104, 119
bicycle travel, *see cycling*
Biodôme 77–8
Biosphère 50–3
boat travel 46, 135, 140
bookstores 71, 81, 95
budgeting 21, 29, 155, 157
bus travel 24–6
business hours 157, 163

C

cabaret 82
Cabaret Mado 31, 82

cafes, *see Drinking subindex*
calling codes 163
canoeing, kayaking & rafting 119, 122, 151
car travel 24, 26
Carnaval de Québec 22, 138
Casa del Popolo 109
cathedrals 68
cemeteries 96
Centre Bell 65
Centre Canadien d'Architecture 121
Chapelle Notre-Dame-de-Bon-Secours 44–5
Château Dufresne 83
Château Frontenac 135–6
Château Ramezay 45
children, traveling with 15, 154
Chinatown, *see Downtown & Chinatown*
Chinatown gate 63
chocolatiers & confectioners 63, 71, 83, 144, 147, *see also maple syrup*
churches, chapels & basilicas, *see also monasteries*
  Basilique Notre-Dame 38
  Basilique-Cathédrale Notre-Dame-de-Québec 133, 137
  Chapelle Notre-Dame-de-Bon-Secours 44–5
  Église St-Jean 146
  Église St-Pierre-Apôtre 81
  Notre-Dame-de-la-Défense 110
  Notre-Dame-du-Sacré-Coeur-Chapel 38
  Oratoire St-Joseph 120
Cimetière Notre-Dame-des-Neiges 96
cinemas 41, 82
Cinémathèque Québécoise 82
Cirque du Soleil 40
climate 22–3

climbing 149
clothes 20
clubs 157
comedy 65
confectioners, *see chocolatiers & confectioners*,
costs 21, 27, 155, 157
credit cards 156
Croisières AML 135, 141
cruises 135
culinary experiences 14, *see also Eating subindex, festivals & events*
currency 21
cycling 26
  Île de la Visitation 104
  Parc Jean-Drapeau 53,
  Québec City 138–9
  tours 118

D

dangers 159
daphne 109
disabilities, travelers with 27, 162
discounts 21, 26
Downtown & Chinatown 55–71, **60, 62**
  drinking 70–1
  food 69–70
  shopping 71
  top experiences 58–9
  transportation 55
  walking tours 60–1, 62–3, **60, 62**
drinking, *see Drinking subindex, wineries*

E

Église St-Jean 146
electricity 163
emergencies 163
entertainment, *see art, ballet, cinemas, comedy, festivals & events, films, music festivals, operas*
Escalier Casse-Cou 31, 134

etiquette 20
EXMURO 31, 140
Expo 67 53

F

Fairmount Bagel 108
family travel 15, 154
Farine Five Roses sign 119
Festival d'été de Québec 139
Festival international de Jazz de Montréal 22, 31, 64
festivals & events 22–3, 31
    Festival d'été de Québec 139
    Festival international de Jazz de Montréal 22, 31, 64
    Fête nationale du Québec 139
    Fierté Montréal 22
    Francos 65
    Just for Laughs 23, 65
    Les Premiers Vendredis 76
    L'International des Feux Loto-Québec 52–3
    Montréal en Lumière 65
    Osheaga 50–1
    Piknic Électronik 50–1
    Semaine de la Poutine festival 140
    Sommets du Cinéma d'Animation 82
    Suoni Per Il Popolo 23
Fierté Montréal 22
films 41, 46, 82
First Nations, *see* indigenous peoples
Fonderie Darling 46
food, drink & nightlife 156–7, *see also* Eating subindex
Fortifications of Québec 130
free experiences 15
French language 164–5

G

gardens 6, *see also individual gardens, parks*
gay travelers 22, 158
Glissade de la Terrasse 138
Grand Quai 41
Grande Roue de Montréal 39–40
Grands Ballets Canadiens 64
green spaces 6, *see also individual gardens, parks*

H

Habitat 67 120, 131
health 159
highlights 6–15
history, *see also* indigenous peoples, natural history
    Catholicism 44, 123, 137
    colonial 66, 123, 150
    Irish 140–1
    Jewish 123
    Prohibition 66
    Révolution Tranquille 136
    Samuel de Champlain 135
    Sir George-Étienne Cartier 45
    St Lawrence River 47
hockey 64–5
Holt Renfrew Ogilvy 61–2
HoMA, *see* Quartier Latin, the Village & HoMA
hostels 155
Hôtel de Ville 43
Hôtel-Musée Premières Nations 150
hotels 155

I

ice climbing 149
ice skating 53, 94–5
Igloofest 23, 40, 139
Île de la Visitation 31, 104–5
Île d'Orléans 146–7
indigenous peoples
    culture 59, 66, 109, 150
    history 131, 150
Insectarium 79–80
insurance 159
Irish Memorial National Historic Site 140
itineraries 16–19

J

Jardin Botanique 79
Just for Laughs 23, 65

K

kayaking, *see* canoeing, kayaking & rafting

L

La Citadelle 139
La Ronde 52–3
Lac aux Castors 90, 96
Lachine Canal & Southwest Montréal 115–25, **116–117**

    cycling tours 118–19, **118**
    drinking 125
    food 124
    shopping 125
    transportation 115
language 20–1, 164–5
Le Monastère 65
Le Monastère des Augustines 137
Le Petit Dep 28, 47, 49, 144
Leonard Cohen 93, 96
LGBTIQ+ travelers 22, 158
Lieu Historique de Sir George-Étienne Cartier 45
Limoilou 141
L'International des Feux Loto-Québec 39, 52–3
Little Italy, *see* Mile End, Little Italy & Outremont
Little Portugal 94

M

Maison Alcan 61
Maison de la littérature 142
Maison Lady Meredith 61
Maison St-Gabriel 123
Manoir Mauvide-Genest 146
maple syrup 29–30
markets & *marchés*, *see individual locations*
Marché Atwater 119, 120
Marché Bonsecours 47
Marché Jean-Talon 110
measurements 163
MEM 66
Métro travel 25
Mile End, Little Italy & Outremont 101–13, **102–3**
    drinking 112
    food 111, 112
    shopping 113
    top experiences 104–5
    transportation 101
    walking tour 106–7, **106**
monasteries 65, 137
money 21
monuments, *see* statues, towers & monuments
Morrin Centre 31, 142
Mount Royal Club 61
Mount Stephen 61
MURAL Festival 23
murals 81, 92–3

167

Musée de Lachine 119
Musée de la Civilisation 131
Musée de L'Holocauste 123
Musée des Ondes Emile Berliner 122–3
Musée des Plaines d'Abraham 134
Musée du Montréal Juif 107
Musée et Centre d'art de Montréal 121
Musée Huron-Wendat 150
Musée Maritime de L'Île d'Orléans 146
Musée McCord Stewart 66
Musée National des beaux-arts du Québec 140
Musée Redpath 67
museums 10, 15, see also *individual locations*
music festivals 22, 23, 91

natural history 67
nature & wildlife 6, 76–9, 104–5
nightlife, see food, drink & nightlife, Drinking subindex, *individual locations*

Observatoire de la Capitale 141
Old Montréal 35–49, **36**
drinking 49
food 48
shopping 49
top experiences 38–41
transportation 35
walking tour 42–3, **42**
Old Port 39–41
opening hours 157, 163
Opéra de Montréal 64
operas 64
Oratoire St-Joseph 120
Outremont, see Mile End, Little Italy & Outremont

🅿
Parc de la Chute-Montmorency 148–9
Parc du Mont-Royal 90–1
Parc du Portugal 94
Parc Jean-Drapeau 50–3, **52**
Parc La Fontaine 94

Parc-nature de l'Île-de-la-Visitation 104–5
Parc Olympique & Espace pour la vie 76–9
Parc René-Lévesque 119
Parc-nature de l'Île-de-la-Visitation 104–5
parks & gardens 6, see also *individual gardens, parks*
Patin Patin 95
pavilions, see walkways & pavilions
Petit Navire 46
Petit-Champlain 134
PHI 46
Place d'Armes 43
Place de la Grande-Paix-de-Montréal 43
Place des Arts 64
Place des Festivals 31
Place d'Youville 43, 137–8
Place Jacques-Cartier 43
Plage de Verdun 122
Plage Jean-Doré 51–5
Plaines d'Abraham 130, 134
Planétarium 78
planning 20–1
plants, see nature & wildlife
plages, see beaches & *plages*
Plateau Mont-Royal 87–99, **88–9**
drinking 98
food 97–8
shopping 99
top experiences 90–1
transportation 87
walking tour 92–3, **92**
Pointe-à-Callière 44
politics 136
population 163
Porte St-Louis 133
poutine 140
public holidays 163
public transportation 26–7

🆀
Quai Jacques-Cartier 40
Quai King Edward 41
Quartier Latin, the Village & HoMa 73–85, **74**
drinking 84–5
food 84
shopping 85

top experiences 76–9
transportation 73
walking tour 80–1, **80**
Québec City 127–45, **128–9**
drinking 144–5
experiences 134–42
food 143–4
shopping 145
top experiences 130–1
transportation 127
walking tour 132–3, **132**

rafting see canoeing, kayaking & rafting
rapids 105
religious buildings, see churches, chapels & basilicas, monasteries, synagogues
Réseau de la Ville Souterraine (RÉSO) 68
responsible travel 160–1
rideshares 24, 26
Robin des Bois 95
Rue du Trésor 133
Rue Notre-Dame 43
Rue St-Paul 47

🆂
safe travel 159
Schwartz's 94
science 41, 78
sculptures, see statues, towers & monuments
shopping, see *individual locations*, Shopping subindex
skiing 53, 94–5
SkySpa 141
snow shoeing 53
Société des Arts Technologiques 67
Southwest Montréal, see Lachine Canal & Southwest Montréal
spas 46–7, 141
speakeasies 144–5
Big in Japan 98
Cloakroom 70
Sans Soleil 69
sports, see *individual activities*

Square Dorchester 68–9
St Lawrence River 47, 122
Stade Olympique 76
statues, towers & monuments
    Cartier Monument 90
    Croix du Mont-Royal 91
    Downtown & Chinatown 68
    Montréal Tower 76
    Port of Montréal Tower 41
    Silo No. 5 41
    Sir Georges-Étienne Cartier Monument 91
    Tour de l'Horloge 39
St-Jean-Baptiste 141
street experiences 13
St-Roch 141
St-Viateur Bagel 108
synagogues 107

T

taxis 24, 26
Terrasse Dufferin 130, **133**, **138**
Théâtre de Verdure 94
theme parks, *see* amusement & adventure parks
time zones 21, 163
tipping 21
TOHU 109
tours, *see also* walking tours
    Downtown & Chinatown 65
    Lachine Canal & Southwest Montréal 120
    Mile End, Little Italy & Outremont 108
    Old Montréal 46
    Parc de la Chute-Montmorency 148–9
    Plateau Mont-Royal 92
    Quartier Latin, the Village & HoMa 83
    Québec City 134–5, 138–40, 142
towers, *see* statues, towers & monuments
train travel 24
transportation 24–7, *see also individual locations*
travel seasons 22–3

U

Underground City 68

V

Vignoble Isle de Bacchus 147
vegetarian & vegan travelers 70, 77, 84, 98, 112, 144
Village, the, *see* Quartier Latin, the Village & HoMa

W

walking 25
walking tours
    Downtown & Chinatown 60, 62, **60**, **62**
    Old Montréal 42, **42**
    Plateau Mont-Royal 92, **92**
    Quartier Latin, the Village & HoMa 80, **80**
    Québec City 132, **132**
walkways & pavilions 13
    Claire & Marc Bourgie Pavilion 58–9
    Jean-Noël Desmarais Pavilion 58–9
    Michael & Renata Hornstein Pavilion 59
    Pavillon du Lac aux Castors 90
    Terrasse Dufferin 130
water, drinking 159
water parks 51–2
waterfalls 148–9, 150
weather 22–3
Wendake 150
Wiggle Room 31, **96**
wildlife, *see* nature & wildlife
wineries 147
winter experiences 8

Z

ziplines 41, 148

Eating

A

Alati-Caserta 110
Alma 111
Améa Cafe 61
Arepera 97
Arthurs 124
Au Pied de Cochon 97
Aube Boulangerie 83
Aube Café 59
Aux Anciens Canadiens 143

B

Bati Cantine 144
Beautys 107
Bernie Beigne 111
Bleu & Persillé 98
Bloom Sushi 70
Blossom 84
Boulangerie Première Moisson 121
Brulerie aux Quatre Vents 121

C

Cadet 69
Café Apotek 143
Café Aunja 69
Cafe Chez Téta 97
Cafe de Course 105
Café du Monde 143
Café Ma Bicyclette 119
Cafe Notman 67
Cafe Parvis 70
Café San Gennaro 110
Café SAT 67
Café Sfouf 84
Caffè Italia 110
Caffettiera 69
Candide 124
Cheskie's 111
Chez Claudette 111
Chez Gaston 143
Chez Temporel 144
Chocolaterie de l'Île d'Orléans 147
Ciccio's 48
Crew Collective & Café 43

D

Dandy 48
Délices de la Mer 110
Dragon Beard Candy 63
Drogheria Fine 108

E

Espace Végo 77
État de Choc 111

F

Fairmount Bagel 107, 108
Fame 108–9
Fleur et Cadeaux 69
Foiegwa 124
Foxy 124
Fromagerie de la Ferme 110

H
Havre-aux-Glaces 110
Hoang Oanh 63
Hof Kelsten 107

J
Janine Café 124
Joe Beef 124

K
Kamùy 69
Kitano Shokudo 98

L
La Banquise 97
La Bûche 143
La Fournée des sucreries de l'érables 110
La Graine Brûlée 84
La Maison de Thé 147
La Maison Smith 143
La Panzeria 97
La Poule Mouillée 97
Lapin Sauté 144
Larrys 111
Le Billig 143
Le Butterblume 111
Le Café Big Trouble 84
Le Cathcart 69
Le Central 69
Le Chic Shack 143
Le Don 144
Le Festigoût Cafe 104
Le Hobbit 143
Le Kahéra 112
Le Lutin Qui Rit 142
Le Petit Dep 49, 144
Le Red Tiger 84
Le Super Qualité 112
Le Taj 70
Le Toledo 98
Le Vivoir 137
L'Express 97
Les Cochons tout Ronds 110
Les Street Monkeys 124
Lloydie's 108
L'Orignal 48

M
Maison Smith 90, 91
Manoir Montmorency 149
Marché Bagels on Greene 124
Marché Jean-Talon 104

Marché Maisonneuve 83
Marci 111
Marion Tavern 84
Mintar 69
Modavie 48
Momo 98
Monarque 48
Mono 59
Montréal Plaza 111
Montréal Pool Room 70

N
Noodle Factory 63
Nora Gray 69

O
Olive et Gourmando 48
Othym 84

P
Patati Patata 97
Pâtisserie Bao Bao Dim Sum 63
Pâtisserie Coco 63
Pavillon du Lac aux Castors 91
Perogie Lili 108
Pichai 112

Q
Qantu 83
Qing Hua Dumplings 63

R
Racer Cafe de Course 105
Restaurant Chinatown Kim Fung 63
Restaurant La Traite 151
Rita 125
Robin des Bois 95

S
Satay Brothers 124
Stash Café 48
Ste-Hélène Bistro-Terrasse 51
St-Viateur Bagel 108

T
Time Out Market 69
Titanic 48
Toqué! 48

U
Upstairs Jazz Bar & Grill 64

V
Vin Mon Lapin 111

W
Wilensky's Light Lunch 107
Wolf & Workman 48

Y
Yokato Yokabai 97

Drinking

A
Aigle Noir 85
Atwater Cocktail Club 125
Au 1884 138

B
Bar Dominion 71
Bar George 61
Bar Henrietta 113
Bar Pamplemousse 71
Bar Vivar 98
BENELUX Brasserie Artisanale 125
Big in Japan 98
Bisou Bisou 49
Bistro à Jojo 85
Bon Délire 125
Brasserie Dieu du Ciel 113
Brasserie Harricana 113
Brasseurs du Monde 84
Buvette Pastek 49

C
Café Alphabet 112
Café Bravo 112
Café des Habitudes 112
Café Tranquille 70
Chez Mère Grand 49
Cloakroom 70
Club Pelicano 70
Coldroom 49
Côte Café 70

E
Érico 144

F
Ferlucci 112

Grumpys Bar 71

JJacques 144
Justine 144

L
La Finca 70
La Korrigane 144
Le Cheval Blanc 84
Le Drague 144–5
Le Petit Dep 49, 144
Le Projet 145
Le Rouge-Gorge 98
Le Sacrilège 145
L'Espace Public 83
L'Oncle Antoine 144

M
Majestique 98
Mamie 113
Mellön 113
Messorem 125
Milky Way Cocktail Bar 125
Motel Motel 85

N
North Star Machines 98

O
Osmo x Murasan 70

P
Pastel Rita 112
Poincaré 70–1
Polari 112
Projet Pilote 98

R
Renard 81, 85
Réservoir 98

S
Saloon 85
Sans Soleil 70
Stereo 85
Stud 85

T
Tommy Café 49
Turbo Haüs 85

Verdun Beach Wine Bar 125
Vinvinvin 112

Zab 104
Zab Café 112

Shopping

Affiche en Tête 99
Annex Vintage 113
Antiquités Bolduc 145
Artgang 93
Artisans Canada 145
Artpop 99
atelier b 113
Au Papier Japonais 113
Aux Quatre Points Cardinaux 85
Ave Duluth 95

Boutique de Noël 145

C
Cafe Camas 99
Camellia Sinensis 85
Candylabs 125
Chocolaterie de l'Île d'Orléans 147
Coeur de Loup 145

De Stiil 95
Divine Chocolatier 71
Drawn & Quarterly 113

Éditions Galerie l'Imagerie 145
Eva B 71
Ex-Voto 113

Fromagerie Atwater 85

Galerie d'art Inuit Brousseau 145

GanK 125
GG & M Bourguet Antiquités 145

Harricana 125
Henri Henri 71
Holt Renfrew Ogilvy 61

Indiana Jeans 71

La Caravane Vintage 99
La Grande Ours 95
La Maison Simons 71
La Petite Cabane à sucre du Québec 145
L'Affichiste 49
Le Cartel 99
Le Grand Marché 145
Le Magasin Général Lambert Gratton 95
L'Empreinte Coopérative 47
Les Chocolats de Chloé 95
L'Euguélionne 81
Livart 99
L'Original 47, 99

Marché Floh 99
Marché Saint Laurent 49
Multimags 99

Palmo Goods 99
Pantalons Supérieur 71
PONY 113
Priape 81

Sacred Fire Productions 49

Wachiya 49
Word , The 71

Send Us Your Feedback

We love to hear from travelers – your comments help make our books better. We read every word, and we guarantee that your feedback goes straight to the authors. Visit lonelyplanet.com/contact to submit your updates and suggestions.

Note: We may edit, reproduce and incorporate your comments in Lonely Planet products such as guidebooks, websites and digital products, so let us know if you are happy to have your name acknowledged. For a copy of our privacy policy visit lonelyplanet.com/legal.

Acknowledgments

Cover photograph: Montréal, QC, Canada. Ally Griffin/Unsplash

Back photograph: Belvédère Kondiaronk. Shawn.ccf/Shutterstock

THIS BOOK

This guidebook was produced by:

Destination Editor
Caroline Trefler

Coordinating Editor
Simon Richmond

Cartographer
Julie Sheridan

Production Editor
Ursula O'Sullivan-Dale

Image Editor
Dorota Mihelac

Assisting Editors
Peterjon Cresswell, Melanie Dankel, Kate James

Cover Researchers
Giada de Agostinis, Gwen Cotter

Thanks to Pamela MacNaughtan, Robert Isenberg, Saralinda Turner, Darren O'Connell

Although the authors and Lonely Planet have taken all reasonable care in preparing this book, we make no warranty about the accuracy or completeness of its content and, to the maximum extent permitted, disclaim all liability arising from its use.

All rights reserved. No part of this publication may be copied, stored in a retrieval system, or transmitted in any form by any means, electronic, mechanical, recording or otherwise, except brief extracts for the purpose of review, and no part of this publication may be sold or hired, without the written permission of the publisher. Lonely Planet and the Lonely Planet logo are trademarks of Lonely Planet and are registered in the US Patent and Trademark Office and in other countries. Lonely Planet does not allow its name or logo to be appropriated by commercial establishments, such as retailers, restaurants or hotels. Please let us know of any misuses: lonelyplanet.com/legal/intellectual-property.

Paper in this book is certified against the Forest Stewardship Council™ standards. FSC™ promotes environmentally responsible, socially beneficial and economically viable management of the world's forests.

Published by Lonely Planet Global Limited
CRN 554153
4th edition – May 2026
ISBN 978 1 83869 905 5
© Lonely Planet 2026
10 9 8 7 6 5 4 3 2 1
Printed in China